OECD Studies on Water

Water Governance in African Cities

Please cite this publication as:
OECD (2021), *Water Governance in African Cities*, OECD Studies on Water, OECD Publishing, Paris, *https://doi.org/10.1787/19effb77-en*.

ISBN 978-92-64-35962-8 (print)
ISBN 978-92-64-71543-1 (pdf)
ISBN 978-92-64-59348-0 (HTML)
ISBN 978-92-64-58309-2 (epub)

OECD Studies on Water
ISSN 2224-5073 (print)
ISSN 2224-5081 (online)

Revised version, June 2021
Details of revisions available at: *https://www.oecd.org/about/publishing/Corrigendum-Water-governance-in-African-cities.pdf*

Photo credits: Cover © gettyimages/Hibrida13.

Corrigenda to publications may be found on line at: *www.oecd.org/about/publishing/corrigenda.htm*.

Preface

The OECD, UCLG –Africa, the World Water Council and the Kingdom of Morocco are delighted to introduce this report on *Water Governance in African Cities.* This report is published as part of the *OECD Programme on Water Security for Sustainable Development in Africa*, launched in 2018 by the OECD Secretary-General Mr Angel Gurría, the recipient of the 6th edition of the King Hassan II Great World Water Prize.

Achieving the Sustainable Development Goal number 6 on "Clean Water and Sanitation" and other water-related targets by 2030, requires that national and local governments put in place the enabling conditions to effectively manage risks of too much, too little or too polluted water, while providing access to water quality services to all. If no action is taken, it is estimated that by 2050, more than 160 million people in Africa will be living in urban areas with a perennial water shortage. The need to address these pressing health and hygiene challenges for the 40% of sub-Saharan African citizens lacking basic access to water supply and the 70% lacking access to basic sanitation, has only been magnified by the COVID-19 pandemic .

Megatrends related to climate change, urbanisation and demographic shifts will further exacerbate pressures on water resources. The African continent is one of the most exposed to climate change impacts. Moreover, between now and 2050, two thirds of on-going urbanisation will happen in towns and intermediary cities, which have less capacity to deploy enabling and mitigating infrastructure than larger ones.

Building on a survey across 36 cities of all sizes in Africa, this report provides a regional analysis of who does what in water management, the effectiveness of institutional, policy and regulatory frameworks, as well as the critical governance gaps that need to be bridged in order to boost the capacity of all towns and cities to drive water security in the African continent. This first ever comprehensive analysis of water governance challenges at the local level in Africa aims not only to raise awareness of pressing and emerging issues that urban areas face, but also to galvanise political action from Mayors and city leaders.

In order to provide momentum to the policy dialogue underlying this report and the evidence it brings, a '*Roundtable of African Mayors for Water Security'* - is being launched as a Policy Forum to share best practices and guide policy reforms and actions on the road to the 9th World Water Forum, to be held in Dakar, Senegal in March 2022. We invite all African mayors to join this platform as a signal of their commitment to the water cause and of their political impetus to improve local water policies for better urban residents' well-being.

Angel Gurria OECD Secretary-General	Abdelkader Amara Minister of Equipment, Transport, Logistics and Water, Morocco	Jean-Pierre Elong Mbassi Secretary-General of UCLG-Africa	Loic Fauchon President of the World Water Council

Foreword

Water Governance in African Cities adds to the rich compendium of country, region, city and thematic reviews published as part of the *OECD Studies on Water* over the past 15 years. This special focus on African cities contributes to the expansion of the global outreach of the OECD's work, thus adding to regional analyses of water governance in OECD countries (2011), Latin America and the Caribbean (2012) and Asia-Pacific (2020), as well as national water governance policy dialogues in Mexico (2013), The Netherlands (2014), Jordan (2015), Tunisia (2015), Brazil (2015 and 2017), Argentina (2019) and Peru (2021).

The regional spotlight on Africa contributes to the preparatory process of the 9th World Water Forum to be held in Dakar, Senegal (March 2022), in which the OECD co-leads the "Implementation Means and Tools" Priority. This report is also an output from the OECD Programme on *Water Security for Sustainable Development in Africa*, launched in 2018 by the OECD Secretary General; the recipient of the 6th edition of the *King Hassan II Great World Water Prize*, during the 8th World Water forum in Brasilia, Brazil (March 2018).

The focus on cities of all sizes aims to raise action from local leaders in driving water security in a continent subject to fast urbanisation. The report emphasises the essential role of cities to improve water governance systems that can secure the effective, efficient and inclusive provision of drinking water and sanitation to all citizens but also to manage mounting challenges related to floods, droughts and water pollution in a shared responsibility with national governments.

Mayors and city leaders, who are closer to citizens and place-based needs, can significantly contribute to the management of water at the appropriate scale, while increasing trust in public policy, through engagement with all stakeholders. This report and the resulting *Mayors' Roundtable for Water Security in Africa* seek to accelerate action at all levels to reach SDG n°6 on "clean water and sanitation" in the continent, and beyond.

This publication contributes to the work of the Regional Development Policy Committee (RDPC). It was approved by RDPC delegates via written procedure on 18 February 2021 under the cote CFE/RDPC(2021)2.

Acknowledgements

This report was prepared by the OECD Centre for Entrepreneurship, SMEs, Regions and Cities (CFE) led by Lamia Kamal-Chaoui, Director, as part of the Programme of Work and Budget of the Regional Development Policy Committee. This report is an output from the OECD Programme on *Water Security for Sustainable Development in Africa*, launched in 2018 by the OECD Secretary-General and developed in cooperation with the Kingdom of Morocco and the World Water Council, as a follow-up to the 6th edition of the King Hassan II Great World Water Prize.

Maria Salvetti, Water Economist and Policy Analyst in the OECD Water Governance Programme, co-ordinated the overall policy dialogue under the supervision of Aziza Akhmouch, Head of the Cities, Urban Policies and Sustainable Development Division in the CFE. Oriana Romano, Head of the Water Governance Programme, CFE and Juliette Lassman, Junior Policy Analyst in the CFE, contributed with comments on the report and substantive inputs. Arthur Minsat, Head of the Europe, Middle East and Africa Unit provided comments on earlier drafts.

The OECD Secretariat is grateful for the support and commitment from United Cities and Local Governments (UCLG) of Africa in conducting the OECD survey on water governance and providing comments on the draft report, in particular: Jean-Pierre Elong Mbassi, Secretary-General; Mohamed Nbou, Director of the Climate, Biodiversity and Food Security Department, Head of the Climate Task Force; Soumia Benlebsir, Project Manager for Stakeholder Mobilisation and Territorialisation of National Contributions; and Nisrine Bennani, Project Manager for Climate Finance Mobilisation.

Special thanks are herein conveyed to the cities that took part in the survey on water governance: Abidjan (Côte d'Ivoire); Abuja (Nigeria); Accra (Ghana); Al Hoceima (Morocco); Antananarivo (Madagascar); Bama (Burkina Faso); Bangangte (Cameroon); Bangui (Central African Republic); Banjul (Gambia); Bobo-Dioulasso (Burkina Faso); Brazzaville (Congo Republic); Cape Town (South Africa); Chefchaouen (Morocco); Cocody (Côte d'Ivoire); Cotonou (Benin); Dakar (Senegal); Dionaba (Mauritania); Fes (Morocco); Golf 3 (Togo); Kampala (Uganda); Kanembakache (Niger); Lome (Togo); Lusaka (Zambia); Maputo (Mozambique); Marrakech (Morocco); Mbour (Senegal); Meknes (Morocco); Monrovia (Liberia); Nouakchott (Mauritania); Rabat (Morocco); Rosso (Mauritania); Saint-Louis (Senegal); Tanger (Morocco); Tetouan (Morocco); Thies (Senegal); and Vogan (Togo).

Furthermore, the draft report benefitted from comments and feedback from: Kevin Collins, Senior Lecturer Environment and Systems at the Open University; Colin Herron, Senior Water Resources Management Specialist at the Global Water Partnership; Donal O'Leary, Senior Advisor at Transparency International; Debjyoty Mukherjee, Principal Public-Private Partnership (PPP) Finance Specialist at the African Bank of Development; Barbara Schreiner, Executive Director at the Water Integrity Network; and Rob Uijterlinde from the Dutch Water Authorities.

Earlier drafts of this report were discussed at two webinars with survey respondents and key stakeholders held on 17 September 2020 and 1 March 2021. Interim findings were also presented at the 14th meeting of the OECD Water Governance Initiative (2-3 November 2020). The report was submitted for approval by written procedure to the Regional Development Policy Committee on 18 February 2021 under the cote CFE/RDPC(2021)2. Special thanks are extended to Pilar Philip for preparing the report for publication and to Eleonore Morena for editing and formatting the report.

Table of contents

FIGURES

TABLES

BOXES

Follow OECD Publications on:
http://twitter.com/OECD_Pubs
http://www.facebook.com/OECDPublications
http://www.linkedin.com/groups/OECD-Publications-4645871
http://www.youtube.com/oecdilibrary
OECD Alerts
http://www.oecd.org/oecddirect/

Abbreviations and acronyms

AMCOW	African Ministers' Council on Water
CCVI	Climate Change Vulnerability Index
CFA	African Financial Community
CICOS	International Commission for the Congo-Oubangui-Sangha Basin
EAC	East African Community
EM-DAT	Emergency Events Database
GDP	Gross domestic product
ICT	Information and communication technologies
IPCC	Intergovernmental Panel on Climate Change
IWRM	Integrated water resources management
KCCA	Kampala Capital City Authority
KWSF	Kampala Water and Sanitation Forum
LICSU	Low-Income Customer Support Unit
LuWSI	Lusaka Water Security Initiative
LYDEC	*Lyonnaise des Eaux Casablanca*
NWASCO	National Water Supply and Sanitation Council
NWSC	National Water and Sewerage Corporation
ODA	Official development assistance
OECD	Organisation for Economic Co-operation and Development
OMVS	Organisation for the Development of the Senegal River (*Organisation pour la mise en valeur du fleuve Sénégal*)
ONEA	National Office of Water and Sanitation (*Office National de l'Eau et de l'Assainissement*)
SDG	Sustainable development goal
SONES	National Water Company of Senegal (*Société Nationale des Eaux du Sénégal*)
UCLG Africa	United Cities and Local Governments Africa
UN	United Nations
UNCTAD	United Nations Conference on Trade and Development
UN DESA	United Nations Department of Economic and Social Affairs
UNDP	United Nations Development Programme
UN-Habitat	United Nations Human Settlements Programme
UNICEF	United Nations International Children's Emergency Fund
USAID	United States Agency for International Development
VAT	Value-added tax
WASH	Water sanitation and hygiene
WHO	World Health Organization
WSS	Water supply and sanitation
WWG	Water Watch Group

Executive summary

COVID-19 has acted as a magnifying glass on pressing water and sanitation challenges in African cities, stressing and widening inequalities for the 56% of the urban population living in informal settlements and relying on shared toilet facilities and public water points for basic handwashing facilities. With about 100 000 COVID-19 related deaths as of February 2021, according to available statistics, Africa is not the hardest-hit continent but African cities, alongside national governments, with higher population densities and large numbers of crowded places such as markets and public transport, have been acutely affected by the need for policy action to contain the spread of the virus.

Before the pandemic, African countries and cities were already facing mounting water challenges. In Sub-Saharan Africa, for example, 40% of people lack basic access to water supply and 70% to basic sanitation, in addition to challenges from concomitant floods, droughts and pollution. More specifically, in urban areas of sub-Saharan Africa, only 20% have access to safely managed sanitation and 25% to basic sanitation, with significant variations across countries. According to Joint Monitoring Programme reporting, in 2017, only 9% of the urban population in Liberia had access to safely managed water services compared to 99% in South Africa, and these gaps have been growing since 2000. In addition to longstanding scarcity challenges, floods are the most frequent and widespread water-related disaster in Africa, particularly in Sub-Saharan Africa where 654 floods affected 38 million people over the last 33 years. In African cities, flood risks (whether flash pluvial, costal or fluvial) are exacerbated by rapid urbanisation, uncontrolled urban growth and unregulated informal settlements on low-lying floodplain areas. Contaminated water is another major issue in Africa: every hour, an estimated 115 people die from diseases related to improper hygiene, poor sanitation or contaminated water.

In addition to the ongoing economic transformation of Africa, megatrends related to climate change, urbanisation and population growth add pressure on water resources. It is estimated that the total number of people living in urban areas with a perennial water shortage will increase to 162 million by 2050. Moreover, Africa is among the most vulnerable continents to climate change, with projected temperatures expected to rise faster than the global average throughout the 21st century and two-thirds of African cities at "extreme" risk of climate-related shocks; exacerbated by high population growth (4% per annum) and poor urban infrastructure. No less than 86 of the 100 fastest-growing cities in the world are located in Africa most of which are sprawling extensively. Between now and 2050, two thirds of on-going urbanisation will happen in towns and intermediary cities, which have less capacity to deploy infrastructure than larger cities. In such a context, reaching the United Nations Sustainable Development Goal (SDG) 6 on "clean water and sanitation" in order to leave no-one behind, is a daunting task, especially when proper water governance conditions are not in place.

As set out in the OECD Principles on Water Governance, coping with current and future water challenges requires robust public policies targeting measurable objectives in predetermined timeframes at the appropriate scale and relying on a clear assignment of duties across responsible authorities and subject to regular monitoring and evaluation. Water governance can greatly contribute to the design and implementation of such policies, in a shared responsibility across national, regional, basin and local levels but also in co-operation with civil society, businesses and the broader range of stakeholders who have an important role to play to reap the economic, social and environmental benefits of water security.

While water resources management, like many other public policies, remains largely centralised in most African countries, cities usually hold key responsibilities for water services, and have an increasing role to play in driving water security now and in the future. Indeed, city governments hold policy prerogatives to secure the effective, efficient and inclusive provision of drinking water and sanitation as a *local* public service. In addition, mayors and city leaders, who are closer to citizens and place-based needs, could play a more significant role in addressing the mismatch between hydrological and administrative boundaries, through contributing to water resources management within integrated basin systems.

Building on a water governance survey across 36 African cities of all sizes, this report provides a regional overview of the allocation of roles and responsibilities for water management, the existence and implementation of institutional, policy and regulatory frameworks, as well as the critical governance gaps that need to be bridged in order to boost city government capacity to drive water security in the continent.

Key findings of the OECD Survey on Water Governance in African Cities include:

- In a majority of African countries, water policy is driven at the national level by a line ministry often in charge of most regulatory functions, including tariff setting, quality standards definitions and monitoring, and consumer protection and engagement. A large number of African countries have also set up national water service providers, thus further amplifying the national leadership.
- The last decade has seen an increasing leadership of city governments in water policy. In addition to national water policies, a significant share of surveyed cities have adopted dedicated local policies, investment plans and programmes for drinking water and sanitation (75%) and water resource management (42%). A vast majority (80%) of cities that have adopted such local policies report that they contribute to overcoming silos that often generate poor planning, lack of policy coherence and misalignment of incentives.
- Where they exist, local water policies usually facilitate co-ordination with strategic urban development policies such as housing, land use and solid waste, and include social measures and targeted provisions towards vulnerable categories of the population in the form of a guaranteed minimum water volume for basic needs, a social connection fee and/or a social tariff.
- In terms of evaluation and monitoring, half of the surveyed cities were hindered by partial and incomplete water-related data and information to guide policymaking and decision-making..
- All surveyed cities consider the lack of funding as a major obstacle to good water governance, not only because of the limited use and uptake of economic instruments, such as pollution and abstraction charges, but also because between USD 9 billion and USD 14 billion would be needed per year throughout the African continent to achieve water security.
- Less than half of the surveyed cities report the existence of clear procurement processes and budget transparency principles. Corruption remains a significant concern in many countries with Sub-Saharan Africa scoring the lowest in Transparency International's annual Corruption Perceptions Index; although with strong variations across countries.
- Finally, African cities report challenges in engaging with stakeholders in water-related matters due to a lack of funding, time and staff, along with the complexity of the issues at hand. In addition, city governments lack basic knowledge about the stakeholders they should engage with: more than three surveyed cities out of four have not carried out a stakeholder mapping for their water sector. Where such engagement practices exist, they rely on a variety of formal and informal mechanisms including meetings (56%), workshops (44%), citizen committees (42%) and river basin organisations (42%).

1 Water security and key megatrends in African cities

This chapter describes the challenges that African countries and cities are facing to address water risks (water abundance and floods, insufficient access to water and sanitation, water pollution, and water scarcity and droughts), manage stakes and strengthen water security. It then underlines how megatrends including climate change, urbanisation and demographic changes are exacerbating these water risks. Finally, it focuses on the issues that the COVID-19 pandemic brings in terms of water security in African countries.

Key water security challenges in African cities: The state of play

Throughout the world, an increasing number of countries are facing mounting challenges to address water risks and strengthen water security. These bring with them serious implications to meeting societal objectives, such as safe drinking water supply, wastewater management, food and energy security, improved health, sustainable ecosystems, poverty eradication and sustained economic growth. Water scarcity, water disasters and extreme weather events, such as floods and droughts, and failures of climate change mitigation and adaptation, rank as top global risks as assessed in the *World Economic Forum's Global Risks Report* (2020[1]).

The OECD defines water security as the management of four water risks:

- **Risk of shortage and scarcity (including droughts)**: Lack of sufficient water to meet demand (in both the short and long run) for beneficial uses by all water users (households, businesses and the environment).
- **Risk of inadequate quality**: Lack of water of suitable quality for a particular purpose or use.
- **Risk of excess (including floods)**: Overflow of the normal confines of a water system (natural or built) or the destructive accumulation of water over areas that are not normally submerged.
- **Risk of inadequate access to safe water supply and sanitation**: Lack of access to safely managed water and sanitation services (Figure 1.1).

Figure 1.1. A risk-based approach to water security: OECD framework

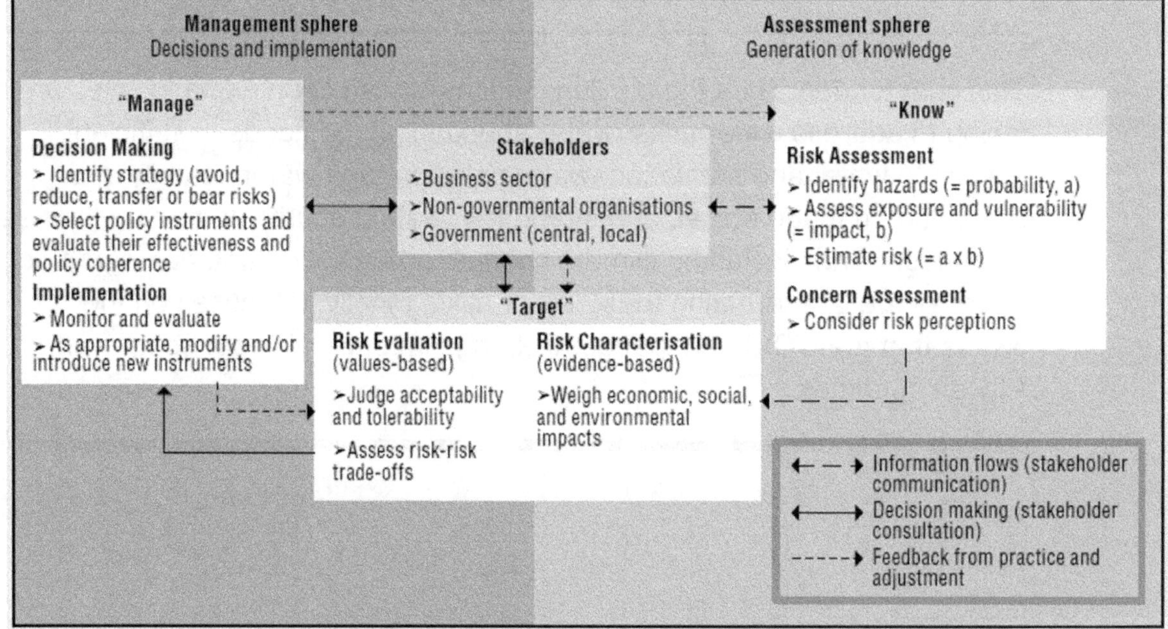

Source: OECD (2013[2]), *Water Security for Better Lives*, http://dx.doi.org/10.1787/9789264202405-en.

In many countries, water security is increasingly put in jeopardy by the effects of climate change, economic growth, urbanisation and demographic patterns, among others. Accessible and high-quality freshwater is a limited and highly variable resource in space and time, and future trends will affect water availability and quality. The OECD projects that by 2050, 40% of the world's population will live in water-stressed river basins and water demand will rise by 55% (OECD, 2012[3]). Flood risks are anticipated to rise rapidly in both OECD countries and non-OECD economies with great potential for the loss of human life and property. Over-abstraction and contamination of aquifers worldwide are posing significant challenges to food security, the health of ecosystems and safe drinking water supply. In addition, by 2050 and despite global efforts, 240 million people are expected to remain without access to clean water and 1.4 billion without access to basic sanitation. Significant investment is required to renew and upgrade infrastructure, estimated at USD 6.7 trillion by 2050 for water supply and sanitation, and including a wider range of water-related infrastructure that could triple that cost by 2030 (OECD, 2015[4]).

The African continent is no exception to these observations as water security is already a major challenge for African countries and cities due to increased water demand tied to population growth, urbanisation and climate change impacts. Demographic trends are pushing water demand up with the African urban population projected to nearly double from more than 560 million in 2015 to 1.1 billion in 2050 (UN, 2015[5])). With 41% of the sub-Saharan African population currently living in cities, and a projected increase to 60% by 2050 (UN, 2015[5]), urbanisation will generate specific challenges related to access to quality drinking water and sanitation services. Climate change is also exacerbating the pressure on water resources with two-thirds of African cities estimated at "extreme risk" with regard to climate change impacts. The amount of gross domestic product (GDP) in African countries exposed to "extreme risk" will grow from USD 895 billion in 2018 to USD 1 397 billion in 2023 (Verisk, Maplecroft, 2018[6]), which represents 48% of the African continent GDP. For instance, in sub-Saharan Africa, the cumulative effect of the last decades indicates that floods and droughts alone are responsible for around 80% of disaster-related deaths and 70% of economic losses (Ndaruzaniye et al., 2010[7]). Damages to infrastructure, property and assets caused by tropical cyclones or flooding are among the more obvious impacts but droughts, crop failure and instability brought by climate change may also move millions of people towards cities through cross-border and rural migration (Verisk, Maplecroft, 2018[6]).

Furthermore, the latest monitoring results of United Nations Sustainable Development Goal (SDG) 6 "Clean water and sanitation" shows that significant or major challenges remain in all African countries, while half of them are showing a stagnating trend towards achieving the various targets associated with SDG 6 (Table 1.1).

Table 1.1. SDG 6 monitoring status and trend in African countries, 2019

	SDG 6 status	SDG 6 trend
	Northern Africa	
Algeria		
Egypt		
Libya		
Mauritania		
Morocco		
Tunisia		
	Western Africa	
Benin		
Burkina Faso		
Cabo Verde		
Cote d'Ivoire		
Gambia		
Ghana		
Guinea		
Guinea-Bissau		
Liberia		
Mali		
Niger		
Nigeria		

	SDG 6 status	SDG 6 trend
Senegal		
Sierra Leone		
Togo		
Eastern Africa		
Burundi		
Comoros		
Djibouti		
Eritrea		
Ethiopia		
Kenya		
Rwanda		
Seychelles		
Somalia		
South Soudan		
Sudan		
Tanzania		
Uganda		
Central Africa		
Cameroon		
Central African Republic		
Chad		
Republic of the Congo		
Democratic Republic of the Congo		
Equatorial Guinea		
Gabon		
Madagascar		
Southern Africa		
Angola		
Botswana		
Eswatini		
Lesotho		
Malawi		
Mauritius		
Mozambique		
Namibia		
Sao Tomé and Principe		
South Africa		
Zambia		
Zimbabwe		

Note:

1. To assess a country's progress status on SDG 6, four bands are considered. The green band is bounded by the maximum that can be achieved for each variable (i.e. the upper bound) and the threshold for achieving the SDG. Three colour bands ranging from yellow to orange and red denote an increasing distance from SDG achievement. The upper and lower bounds are the same as for the index described above.
2. To estimate the SDG 6 trend, linear annual growth rates (i.e. annual percentage improvements) needed to achieve the target by 2030 (i.e. 2010-30) are calculated and compared to the average annual growth rate over the most recent period (e.g. 2015-18). Progress towards SDG 6 achievement is described using a four-colour coding system (e.g. green, yellow, orange and red).

Major challenges remain

Significant challenges remain/Stagnating

Moderately increasing

On track

Source: SDGC/A and SDSN (2020[8]), *Africa SDG Index and Dashboards Report 2020*, Sustainable Development Goals Center for Africa and Sustainable Development Solutions Network.

African cities participating in the OECD Survey on Water Governance carried out over the period of May to September 2020 (Annex A and B) acknowledge their concomitant exposure to many of the above water risks and challenges. Floods and insufficient access to water and sanitation come first as the most prominent challenges to date, followed by other persistent challenges related to water pollution, water scarcity and droughts, ageing water infrastructure, waterborne diseases and, last but not least, water use competition (Table 1.2). The following sections put these water security challenges into perspective to provide a continental overview.

Table 1.2. Key water security challenges in surveyed African cities

Cities	Floods	Insufficient coverage of water and sanitation services	Water pollution	Water scarcity and droughts	Ageing, obsolete infrastructure /lack of infrastructure	Waterborne diseases	Competition/ conflicts over water allocation
Lusaka (Zambia)							
Cape Town (South Africa)							
Kampala (Uganda)							
Monrovia (Liberia)							
Golf 3 (Togo)							
Kanembakache (Niger)							
Saint Louis (Senegal)							
Nouakchott (Mauritania)							
Bangui (Central African Republic)							
Brazzaville (Republic of the Congo)							
Cotonou (Benin)							
Lome (Togo)							
Bama (Burkina Faso)							
Abidjan (Côte d'Ivoire)							
Antananarivo (Madagascar)							
Cocody (Côte d'Ivoire)							
Thies (Senegal)							
Bangangte (Cameroon)							
Vogan (Togo)							
Mbour (Senegal)							
Maputo (Mozambique)							
Abuja (Nigeria)							
Al Hoceima (Morocco)							
Rabat (Morocco)							
Chefchaouen (Morocco)							
Accra (Ghana)							
Dakar (Senegal)							

Cities	Floods	Insufficient coverage of water and sanitation services	Water pollution	Water scarcity and droughts	Ageing, obsolete infrastructure /lack of infrastructure	Waterborne diseases	Competition/ conflicts over water allocation
Marrakech (Morocco)							
Meknes (Morocco)							
Fes (Morocco)							
Tanger (Morocco)							
Tetouan (Morocco)							
Bobo-Dioulasso (Burkina Faso)							
Rosso (Mauritania)							
Dionaba (Mauritania)							
Banjul (Gambia)							

Note: 36 cities responded to the question "Which water risks are the most important in your city?".
Very important
Important
Not important
No answer
Source: OECD (2021[9]), *OECD Survey on Water Governance in African Cities*, OECD, Paris.

Water abundance and floods

Worldwide, floods are affecting 2.5 billion people, representing more than 55% of all fatalities (EM-DAT, 2020[10]) and more than 30% of global economic losses from natural disasters (Hallegatte et al., 2013[11]). Floods are the most frequent and widespread water-related disaster in Africa, particularly in sub-Saharan Africa where 654 floods affected 38 million people in the last 33 years (Tiepolo, 2014[12]). In the past 15 years only, floods and landslides have affected 38 million people in Africa and caused damages estimated to more than USD 4 billion, with Eastern and Western Africa being the most affected regions (Table 1.3).

Table 1.3. Floods and landslides frequency and consequences in Africa from 2005 to 2020

African regions	Number of hydrological disasters	Total days	Total people affected	Total damages (USD thousands)
Eastern Africa	183	1 758	11 754 048	1 093 136
Central Africa	74	622	2 847 250	29 000
Northern Africa	44	583	5 794 534	1 184 100
Southern Africa	24	296	990 643	838 000
Western Africa	124	1 830	17 218 766	1 298 515
Total Africa	**49**	**5 089**	**38 605 241**	**4 442 751**

Source: EM-DAT (2020[10]), *EM-DAT Database*, https://www.emdat.be/database.

In Kampala, Uganda, annual flooding from extreme convective storm rainfalls with an average duration of two hours or more increased from five events in 1993 to ten in 2014 (Douglas, 2017[13]). In Nigeria only, the 2012 flood disasters affected 32 states (on a total of 36) and an estimated total of 7.7 million people (Nkwunonwo, Whitworth and Baily, 2016[14]). More recently, the 2020 East Africa floods affected at least

700 000 people in Burundi, the Democratic Republic of the Congo, Djibouti, Ethiopia, Kenya, Rwanda, Somalia, Tanzania and Uganda.

Flood risks (whether they are flash pluvial, costal or fluvial) in African cities are largely exacerbated by rapid urbanisation, uncontrolled urban growth and unregulated informal settlements in the low-lying floodplain areas. Flash floods result from high-intensity rainfall mostly occurring in steep slopes. Pluvial floods usually happen in urban areas in which drainage system capacity is overwhelmed by intense rainfall (Begum, Stive and Hall, 2007[15]; Houston et al., 2011[16]; Merz, Thieken and Gocht, 2007[17]) (Vojinović, 2015[18]). Fluvial floods are triggered by excessive rainfall over a few hours causing a river to overtop natural or artificial defences and flood urban areas (Vojinović, 2015[18]). Coastal floods usually affect cities that are close to the ocean or the coasts as a result of seasonal storm surges (Vojinović, 2015[18]). The Ogunpa flood disaster that occurred in Ibadan, Nigeria, which led to more than 200 deaths and destroyed assets worth millions of Nigerian Naira, was a combination of flash, fluvial and pluvial flooding (Etuonovbe, 2011[19]).

Urbanisation which amplifies soil sealing in the built environment prevent rainfall from infiltrating into the soil, increasing the rate and volume of runoff during rainfall events. In Kampala, Uganda, the construction of unregulated structures in informal settlements reduced rainfall infiltration significantly, increasing runoff to six times more than what would occur on natural terrain (ActionAid, 2006[20]). While some of the increase is likely due to climate change, it also largely results from land cover change. Thus, even moderate storms produce high flows, with more important and more frequent floods (ActionAid, 2006[20]) (Satterthwaite, 2008[21]).

The urban poor and those living in unplanned urban settlements are disproportionally affected by flooding (see Douglas et al. (2008[22]) for examples) as, for instance, these settlements are commonly built on marginal land including flood-prone areas, as illustrated in cities like Lusaka (Zambia) (Nchito, 2007[23]), Port Elizabeth (South Africa) and Johannesburg (South Africa) (Viljoen and Booysen, 2006[24]). In addition, the poor materials used for construction increase flood damages and fatality in informal settlements (Pharoah, 2014[25]). Frequent floods not only damage properties and result in direct loss of life but also disrupt traffic and expose people to health risks because of exposure to sewage, industrial waste and waterborne disease (Lall, Henderson and Venables, 2017[26]).

Insufficient access to water and sanitation

According to JMP reporting (WHO/UNICEF, 2019[27]), urban access to safely managed piped water ranges from 9% in Liberia to 99% in South Africa, with upward and downward evolution from 2000 to 2017. Downward evolutions underline the difficulties that cities are facing to expand water infrastructure in a context of urban population growth and unplanned urbanisation (Table 1.4). It is estimated that the total number of people living in urban areas with a perennial water shortage will increase from 24 million in 2000 to 162 million by 2050 (McDonald et al., 2011[28]).

Table 1.4. Urban access to piped safely managed water in select African countries, 2000-17

Cities	2000	2017
Benin	67	54
Burkina Faso	82	74
Cameroon	71	61
Central African Republic	49	NA
Republic of the Congo	85	73
Gambia	85	84
Ghana	80	40

Côte d'Ivoire	72	62
Liberia	25	9
Madagascar	59	70
Mauritania	44	66
Morocco	95	94
Mozambique	55	75
Niger	86	83
Nigeria	37	15
Senegal	85	86
South Africa	99	98
Togo	74	45
Uganda	61	53
Zambia	82	68

Source: WHO/UNICEF (2019[27]), "Progress on household drinking water, sanitation and hygiene 2000-17. Special focus on inequalities", World Health Organization and United Nations Children's Fund, New York.

Disparities related to urban water access across African countries are linked with the characteristics of urban habitat; but national averages also mask huge intra-country disparities, within and across cities, and between urban and rural areas, depending on where infrastructure and public services are concentrated. They tend to be mostly located in central and planned areas of African cities, while access to services declines when moving away from city centres. For instance, in Côte d'Ivoire, urban audits in 2013 showed that peri-urban and informal settlements are lacking adequate infrastructure and public services that are on the contrary present in the core of the cities. In Accra, Ghana, access to piped water, waste disposal and toilet facilities decreases as the distance to the city centre increases (Vinay, 2017[29]). The same situation is observed in Maputo, Mozambique.

Population growth and rapid outward urbanisation, among others, are already overwhelming existing urban infrastructure and challenge the capacity of institutions to respond to water demand. Economic growth and the emergence of a middle class with growing water needs will further add to that water demand. This is particularly alarming in a context of climate change and water scarcity. Some African cities are expected to be particularly affected by this evolution, like Bamako (Mali), Kampala (Uganda), Lagos (Nigeria), Niamey (Niger) and Ouagadougou (Burkina Faso) as they are in areas at high risk of water stress (Vörösmarty et al., 2010[30]).

Usually, poor people living in informal settlements have to rely on multiple water sources (e.g. boreholes, rain harvesting, etc.) with increasing health risks due to unsafe drinking water. Nevertheless, some African cities have managed to provide access to improved piped water to poor people.

- For instance, Dakar, Senegal, managed to reach the poorest 40% of the urban population either by connecting individual properties on premises or through public stand posts in the proximity of dwellings (Figure 1.2).
- The city of Cape Town provides free basic water and sanitation services to residents in informal settlements with 1 water tap per 25 families within a radius of 200 metres, and a minimum of 1 toilet per 5 families. As a whole, the city provides and maintains over 10 000 communal standpipes (taps) and over 50 000 toilets regularly cleaned (Box 1.1).

Figure 1.2. Piped water coverage in Dakar, Senegal

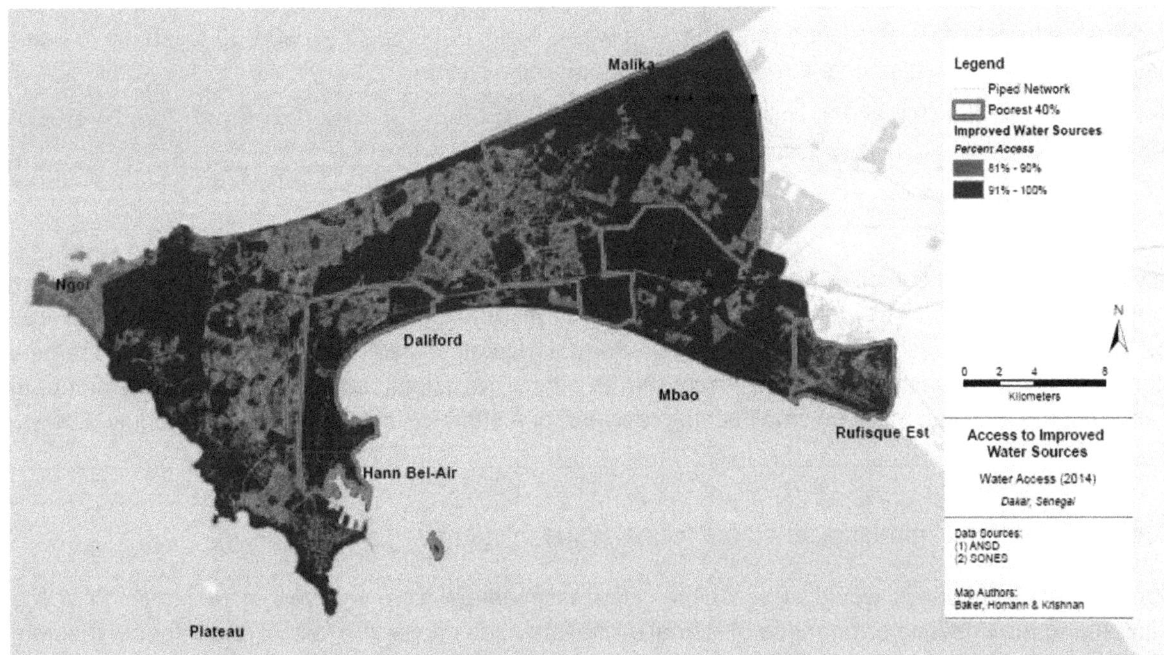

Source: Lall, S.V., J.V. Henderson and A.J. Venables (2017[26]), *Africa's Cities: Opening Doors to the World*, World Bank, Washington, DC.

Box 1.1. Water and sanitation support measures in informal settlements of Cape Town, South Africa

According to South Africa's 2011 Census, 20.5% of Cape Town's households live in informal dwellings – with 7% in informal backyard structures and 13.5% in informal settlements. This proportion is expected to rise steadily as more and more people move to the city looking for work. Urban or peri-urban informal settlements are located nearby urban centres or an economic node, and are characterised by a lack of formal town planning layout and approvals, a lack of formal tenure and informal housing without building plans and related approvals (Housing Development Agency, South Africa, 2014[31]).

There are currently 204 recognised informal settlements in Cape Town comprising 437 individual pockets. These pockets can be large blocks of hundreds of homes, small clusters of only a few homes scattered on land in between formal houses, or individual homes on plots surrounded by food gardens. There is a wide variation in the number of households in a pocket, ranging from 3 in Chris Hani Park pocket to nearly 8 000 in Enkanini pocket. Many of the informal settlements in Cape Town were established before 2000 and are not recognised as permanent, and their residents lack occupation rights and security of tenure. Only 17 pockets (4%) are less than 5 years old, around 286 pockets (65%) were established before the year 2000 and 103 (24%) were established before democracy.

In line with the national government policy, the city of Cape Town provides free basic water and sanitation services to residents in informal settlements with 1 water tap per 25 families within a radius of 200 m, and a minimum of 1 toilet per 5 families. As a whole, the city provides and maintains over 10 000 communal standpipes (taps) and over 50 000 toilets which are regularly cleaned. Most informal settlements have full flush (waterborne) toilets and these are generally preferred by both the city and communities. However, it is not always possible to place flush toilets in areas that are vulnerable to flooding, on unstable ground (e.g. former solid waste disposal sites), on private land or so densely settled that there is no room for water infrastructure. Hence alternative toilets have also been installed comprising, for instance, chemical toilets, portable flush toilets or container toilets. The majority of these non-flush alternatives are cleaned three times a week. From 2006 to 2014, 30 000 toilets have been installed in informal settlements throughout the city of Cape Town.

Source: City of Cape Town (2020[32]), *City of Cape Town Website*; OECD (forthcoming[33]), *Water Governance in Cape Town*, OECD Publishing, Paris.

In a vast majority of African cities, in addition to formal utilities providing access to water, there are several informal water vendors.[1] They tend to fill the gaps left by incomplete or inadequate piped water coverage (Box 1.2). Where there is incomplete coverage, informal markets fill residual needs and where the piped water reliability and quality is low, consumers turn to alternative supply sources. Thus, nearly half of the urban African population relies on small-scale providers for a share of their water supply (Kariuki, 2005[34]).

Box 1.2. Do informal markets crowd out formal water systems?

Conventional economics would suggest that informal markets have evolved in response to policy failures and the uneven performance of formal utilities. In such cases, the formal and informal markets are more likely to be complementary rather than competitors. However, competition (substitutability) could emerge in situations where the formal and informal sectors compete for inputs (access to water) or customers, or where the formal sector colludes with the informal to restrict access and expansion of infrastructure networks, which can drive demand for the informal sector. These are situations where the presence of the informal sector may impede the growth of the formal sector, by reducing demand for or eroding profits of the formal sector. Bottled water markets, for instance, may also lead to lower expectations of water quality from water utilities (Hawkins, 2017[35]).

Where formal and informal markets overlap (as they do for potable water almost universally) – two outcomes may emerge. Consumers may benefit from greater choice and latent competition between the sectors, resulting in perhaps lower prices and better service. Most often such markets become segmented – with private suppliers focusing upon a higher value-added niche – such as "purified" drinking water.

The existing evidence on the effect of informal markets on formal systems is patchy but broadly confirms expectations of economists; informal vendors fill a gap in formal water systems due to coverage, reliability, quality or all of the above. In the case of overlapping informal and formal systems for delivering drinking water, the evidence is less clear. There are examples of latent competition between the formal and informal sector with cases where the informal sector for sachet and bottled water has grown even where piped connections exist. This competition should lead to improved service quality for drinking water but the effect on price is less clear due to the differences between packed and piped water supplies, and the impact of subsidies on tariff structures for formal water systems.

The global experience suggests that the relationship between informal markets and formal water systems can also be complex. Informal markets are linked with formal systems in several ways which can both undermine and strengthen formal systems depending on the circumstances. First, informal vendors often rely on public boreholes for some portion of their water supply. This has led to negotiation, concessions or memoranda of understanding to secure bulk water tariffs for informal vendors.

Interactions between informal and formal systems can exacerbate corruption, including: rent extraction, unofficial taxes by local and public officials and conflicts of interest when government officials operate side businesses as informal vendors. Vendors regularly report conflicts with water utilities and complain that formal systems are ill-equipped to deal with small-scale service providers or see them as competition. Conversely, formal water systems accuse vendors of hostility, violence and vandalism to prevent the expansion of the water network into regions served by informal vendors. Such behaviour throws into question whether the informal sector can offer a transitional or stopgap water supply in fast-growing regions because the expansion of formal water supply networks threatens businesses and jobs tied to informal vending. Such considerations are far from trivial, as experienced in Ghana where the sachet market supports a thriving set of small-scale and industrial water vendors. Vendor associations have established a potential bridge between entities by encouraging co-operation among vendors ((Wutich, 2016[36]), fostering dialogue with utilities and reducing rent-seeking behaviour (Solo, 2003[37]). On the other hand, some consumers are unwilling to pay for piped connections due to limited confidence in the public water systems. In such situations, the proliferation of informal vendors can crowd out government investments in formal water systems due to the low likelihood of recovering costs, creating a vicious cycle.

Source: Garrick, D. et al. (2019[38]), *Informal Water Markets in an Urbanising World: Some Unanswered Questions*, World Bank, Washington, DC; Hawkins G. (2017[35]), *The impacts of bottled water: an analysis of bottled water markets and their interactions with tap water provision*, WIREs Water, 4, 10.1002/wat2.1203; Solo T. M., (2003[37]), Independent Water Entrepreneurs in Latin America: The other private sector in water services. Washington, D.C.: The World Bank; Wutich, Beresford and Carvajal, (2016[36]), *Can Informal Water Vendors Deliver on the Promise of A Human Right to Water? Results From Cochabamba, Bolivia*, World Development, 79, 14-24

In Ouagadougou, Burkina Faso, the National Office of Water and Sanitation (ONEA) does not have a formal mandate to serve informal settlements as dwellers commonly lack legal titles to occupy the land. To overcome this issue, the utility provides water up to a metering point at the limit of the settlement and then has delegated the service provision within the settlement to small-scale providers. These operators either connect individual premises or set up standpipes. ONEA supplies connection materials and reimburses installation costs to informal operators to encourage the expansion of connections. Although informal operators are allowed to sell water at a higher tariff than ONEA, the price they charge is controlled by ONEA to reduce the risk of local monopoly power and excessive tariff level. The tariff policy with regard to standpipe, fountains, buckets or casks supply is published on the ONEA website. In 2015, 7 578 connections had been installed in 5 informal settlements of Ouagadougou (Figure 1.3).

Figure 1.3. Water service provision in informal settlements in Ouagadougou, Burkina Faso

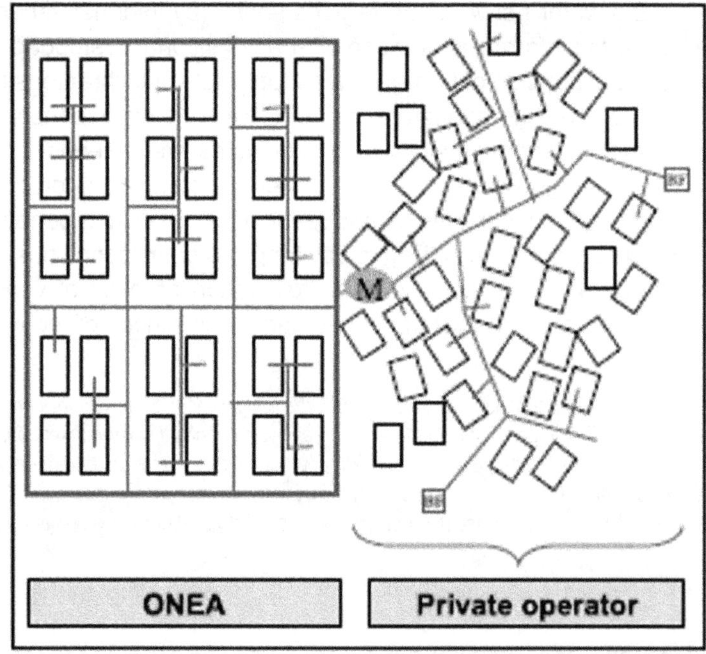

Source: Sawadogo, D. (2015[39]), "Delivering city-wide WASH services: reaching informal settlements in Ouagadougou, Burkina Faso".

In Maputo, 94% of households have access to piped water. The utility Águas da Região de Maputo reports a water coverage rate of 44% of the population, while about 500 small-scale providers manage over 800 piped systems and supply water to 50% of the population mostly through yard taps (Box 1.3).

Box 1.3. The role of small-scale providers in Greater Maputo, Mozambique

The metropolitan area of Maputo has between 1.7 million to 2 million inhabitants. The vast majority of households get their water from a yard tap or house connection. Maputo's 500 or so water operators provide piped water services to about 191 000 households. This is more than the 185 000 households served by Águas da Região de Maputo (the main utility). The small-scale providers range in size, with at least 1 serving 12 000 connections.

The tariffs charged by small-scale providers are higher than those charged by the main utility, averaging MZN 35 per m^3, compared to the main utility's charge of MZN 14 for the first social tariff block, MZN 19 for the next, and MZN 25 thereafter. Water providers developed because of the lack of service and poor reliability of the public provider. Private households drilled boreholes for themselves; some then helped their neighbours and translated this into a larger business serving more people. Small-scale operators now provide competing networks even in areas where a public network already exists. In some areas, the United States Agency for International Development (USAID) survey found that small-scale providers were more reliable, provided a service for longer hours compared with the public provider. More recently, the public provider has experienced difficulties with the adequacy of its water supply and has reduced its hours of supply due to maintenance problems.

The USAID survey also found that small-scale providers offer more flexible terms for payment. For these reasons, many customers prefer using a private provider rather than a public provider even when there is a choice and notwithstanding the higher tariff. Small-scale providers are 100% self-financed.

They are practical in Maputo due to the readily available groundwater found in wide-ranging and shallow aquifers. This is a safe source of water in many, but not all, areas. Risks involve saline intrusion as the water table is lowered through over-extraction and contamination of the source with nitrates and pathogens from human waste as a result of inadequate or poorly maintained sanitation and wastewater infrastructure.

The government has taken the initiative to both recognise and regulate small-scale operators. In areas where groundwater quality is a problem, special regulations will apply and the public provider will sell bulk piped water from the public network to small-scale water providers in these areas. All small-scale providers will need to be licensed in terms of a decree made by the Minister's Council in October 2015, yet to be published and licenses will address issues of mandate (area of service), water quality and price. It is anticipated that this system, in the process of being established, will reduce conflicts between the public and small-scale providers. Licenses will be issued by the local municipalities or district government and the system will be overseen by the national water regulator, CRA. A key challenge will be to establish capacity at the local and district government levels to issue licenses and, for this reason, CRA will provide training and guidance.

Source: USAID (2015[40]), *Sustainable Water and Sanitation for Africa: Final Report.*

In Accra, Ghana, about 80% of residents have access to drinking water, half through piped water into premises and half through private vendors. The latter share has more than tripled, rising from 13.8% in 2010 to 43.1% in 2014 (Guzmán and Stoler, 2018[41]), due to rapid urbanisation combined with underinvestment in infrastructure. The cost of water from informal vendors is generally five to seven times higher than piped water (Vinay, 2017[29]). Informal private vendors distribute water through several mechanisms: half-litre plastic sachets sold in shops and on the streets, tanker services and trucks, and 15- to 20-litre containers.

Water pollution

Contaminated water is a major issue in Africa as every hour an estimated 115 people die from diseases related to improper hygiene, poor sanitation or contaminated water (UN, 2015[5]). Sanitation issues are among the leading causes of disease transmission in Africa, especially for cholera, diarrhoea, dysentery and typhoid. Rapid urbanisation fairly contributes to the deterioration of water quality as cities are struggling to provide adequate wastewater infrastructure to a fast-growing population. In sub-Saharan Africa urban areas, only 20% of the population has access to safely managed sanitation and 25% to basic sanitation (WHO/UNICEF, 2019[27]). According to the World Health Organization (WHO), more than 842 000 deaths are caused each year by a lack of clean water and by poor sanitation.

Monitoring data for SDG 6.3.1 (proportion of wastewater safely treated from households) collected in 2015 are scarce but they showed that the share of wastewater from households treated is very low in sub-Saharan African countries (Niger, Senegal, Somalia and Uganda) compared to high levels in Northern African countries ((UN-Water, n.d.[42])) (Table 1.5). In addition, the limited solid waste management in most African cities is further aggravating the situation through dirty water runoffs.

The ambient quality of water bodies is poorly monitored and only a few African countries are reporting on SDG 6.3.2 (proportion of water bodies with good ambient water quality). This situation underlines that water quality data is either missing or not readily available. This result highlights the crucial need to better monitor water quality to address effectively pollution issues.

Farming also has adverse effects on water quality. The release of important quantities of organic matter, agrochemicals and sediments, and the use of pesticides, fertilisers and excreta cause nitrates and phosphates to infiltrate water bodies leading to eutrophication. Pollution through sediment and nutrient is closely linked to land use changes and practices. In West Africa, deforestation reduced tropical rainfall and affected wildlife, weather patterns and ecosystems. It caused soil erosion, generating more sediment into nearby water bodies. The potential impacts of unchecked land development are expected to increase in the future, with Africa expected to experience the greatest expansion of cropland globally by 2050.

Table 1.5. Monitoring of SDG 6.3.1 (2015) and 6.3.2 (2017) for African countries

Country	SDG 6.3.1 Proportion of wastewater safely treated (%), from households, 2015	SDG 6.3.2 Proportion of water bodies with good ambient water quality (%), 2017
Tunisia	70.57	
Egypt	57.61	
Morocco	42.96	79.15
Algeria	17.75	
Libya	15.25	
Senegal	14.55	
Uganda	3.76	
Niger	3.48	
Somalia	0.7	
Madagascar		90.91
Sudan		86.05
Zimbabwe		76.46
Nigeria		52.46
Botswana		50.00
South Africa		46.92
Kenya		35.50
Rwanda		30.00
Lesotho		16.67
Tanzania		0.00

Source: UN-Water (n.d.[42]), *Indicator 6.3.1 – Wastewater Treatment*, https://www.sdg6data.org/indicator/6.3.1; UN-Water (n.d.[43]), *Indicator 6.3.2 – Water Quality*, https://www.sdg6data.org/indicator/6.3.2.

Emerging pollution issues are likely to substantially increase the needs and costs of wastewater management, in particular in urban environments. These include improvement of individual and other appropriate sanitation systems, combined sewers and risks of overflows, contaminants of emerging concern (such as micro-plastic) or sludge management.

Water scarcity and droughts

Africa is the second-driest continent in the world after Australia. About two-thirds of its territory is arid or semi-arid and more than one-third of the sub-Saharan African population live in a water-scarce environment – with less than 1 000 m^3 per capita per year (UN, 2014[44]). It is estimated that by 2030, 75 to 250 million people in Africa will be living in areas of high water stress, which will likely displace from 24 to 700 million people as living conditions will become increasingly unliveable (Climat, environnement, société, 2012[45]).

Evapotranspiration associated with rising temperatures is likely to increase drought frequencies, as they may cancel out precipitation projected increases in some areas of the continent. For example, in Eastern and Southern Africa, droughts are projected to intensify due to evapotranspiration and precipitation changes (Niang et al., 2014[46]) and will continue to contribute to water scarcity. This finding is further confirmed by the fact that many African countries are considered on a high or extremely high baseline water stress (World Resources Institute, 2019[47]). Among them, are, for instance, Botswana, Namibia or Djibouti (Table 1.6).

Table 1.6. Water stress level per African country, 2019

African countries	Water stress level
Libya	Extremely high (>80%)
Eritrea	Extremely high (>80%)
Botswana	Extremely high (>80%)
Morocco	High (40%-80%)
Algeria	High (40%-80%)
Tunisia	High (40%-80%)
Burkina Faso	High (40%-80%)
Djibouti	High (40%-80%)
Namibia	High (40%-80%)
Niger	High (40%-80%)
Egypt	High (40%-80%)
Sudan	Medium–High (20%-40%)
South Africa	Medium–High (20%-40%)
Mauritania	Medium–High (20%-40%)
Lesotho	Medium–High (20%-40%)
Zimbabwe	Low–Medium (10%-20%)
Angola	Low–Medium (10%-20%)
Tanzania	Low–Medium (10%-20%)
South Sudan	Low–Medium (10%-20%)
Chad	Low–Medium (10%-20%)
Senegal	Low–Medium (10%-20%)
Nigeria	Low–Medium (10%-20%)
Ethiopia	Low–Medium (10%-20%)
Swaziland	Low–Medium (10%-20%)
Somalia	Low–Medium (10%-20%)
Rwanda	Low (<10%)
Guinea-Bissau	Low (<10%)
Mozambique	Low (<10%)
Kenya	Low (<10%)
Zambia	Low (<10%)
Ghana	Low (<10%)
Madagascar	Low (<10%)
Malawi	Low (<10%)
Mali	Low (<10%)
Burundi	Low (<10%)
Uganda	Low (<10%)
Guinea	Low (<10%)
Benin	Low (<10%)
Democratic Republic of the Congo	Low (<10%)
Côte d'Ivoire	Low (<10%)
Cameroon	Low (<10%)

African countries	Water stress level
Gambia	Low (<10%)
Central African Republic	Low (<10%)
Sierra Leone	Low (<10%)
Togo	Low (<10%)
Republic of the Congo	Low (<10%)
Gabon	Low (<10%)
Equatorial Guinea	Low (<10%)
Liberia	Low (<10%)
Comoros	No data
Cape Verde	No data
Mauritius	No data
São Tomé and Príncipe	No data
Seychelles	No data

Note: Water stress is defined as the ratio of withdrawals to supply.
Source: World Resources Institute (2019[47]), *Upward and Outward Growth: Managing Urban Expansion for More Equitable Cities in the Global South.*

The consequences of droughts are manifold. In 2019, failed rains across Eastern Africa, Southern Africa and the Horn of Africa increased food prices and drove up the aid needs of more than 45 million people struggling to find enough food across 14 countries. This same year, in Southern Africa alone, according to the International Federation of Red Cross and Red Crescent Societies (IFRC), at least 11 million people faced food shortages due to drought. Diminished and late rainfall, combined with long-term increases in temperatures, have jeopardised the food security and energy supplies in the region, most acutely in Zambia and Zimbabwe. Grain production was down 30% across the region and 53% in Zimbabwe. Livestock farmers in Southern Africa have also suffered losses due to starvation and to early culling of herds forced by shortages of water and feed. In Kenya, water scarcity induces rural to urban migration, thus increasing pressure on already insufficient urban water supplies (Kinuthia-Njenga, 2009[48]). In Mombasa, Kenya, a drought caused an increase in food prices, disproportionately affecting the urban poor (Awuor, Orindi and Adwera, 2008[49]). In Lusaka, Zambia, following a drought year, urban agricultural output was significantly reduced, thus undermining household food security and income (Simatele, Binns and Simatele, 2012[50]). These examples highlight the various economic, social and health implications of droughts. They also underline the vulnerability of African cities to such water risks.

In 2015, the city of Cape Town started experiencing drought and water reservoirs further reached critically low levels in 2017 and in 2018. The intense hydrological drought attributable to the effects of climate change was exacerbated by anthropic factors such as rising urban population and regional competition among local water users, all placing enormous stress on limited resources. The 16 April 2018 was postulated to be the day that Cape Town switched off its taps. Colloquially termed "Day Zero", this was defined as the point at which the dam levels fell to 13.5%, therefore requiring all taps in the city of Cape Town to be shut off and citizens to fetch a daily 25 litres per person at public points of distribution (PODs). Although Day Zero did not happen, the Cape Town water crisis exposed a serious vulnerability to water scarcity issues for the city of Cape Town, the surrounding urban agglomerations and the country at large. Water scarcity issues put greater pressure on the rural-urban interdependent relationship. The 2015-18 drought had a significant impact on agriculture, livelihoods and communities, with an estimated economic loss of ZAR 5.9 billion (USD 0.4 billion) for agriculture in the Western Cape alone, 30 000 job losses and 13%-20% exports drop (World Wildlife Fund, 2018[51]). Tourism accounts for 10% of South Africa's economic output and provides 1.5 million jobs – around 10% of total employment in the country (Parks, 2019[52]).

Key megatrends affecting African cities

Around the world, a number of economic, social and environmental trends are generating major disruptions now and in the future, and challenging public policies at all levels. The most significant of these are considered megatrends, as they are large in scale and long-term in nature – usually relevant for at least two decades. Consequently, megatrends usually refer to circumstances that will unfold across the globe in a number of countries and that can often drive the global economy and society in specific directions. Megatrends are likely to result in meaningful, long-term changes impacting social, economic, political, environmental and technological issues. Despite their potential for high impact, they often unfold slowly and follow relatively stable trajectories.

In African countries and cities, some of these megatrends significantly affect water security, as is the case of climate change, urbanisation and population growth. Climate change is also exacerbating the pressure on water resources with two-thirds of African cities estimated at "extreme risk" with regard to climate change impacts. For instance, in sub-Saharan Africa, the cumulative effect of the last decades indicates that floods and droughts alone are responsible for around 80% of disaster-related deaths and 70% of economic losses (Ndaruzaniye et al., 2010[7]). With 41% of the sub-Saharan African population currently living in cities, and a projected increase to 60% by 2050 (UN, 2015[5]), urbanisation will exacerbate existing challenges related to access to quality drinking water and sanitation services. And last but not least, demographic trends are pushing water demand up (Figure 1.4) with African urban population projected to nearly double from more than 560 million in 2015 to 1.1 billion in 2050 (UN, 2014[44]).

Figure 1.4. Evolution of water withdrawal in Africa, from 1998 to 2017

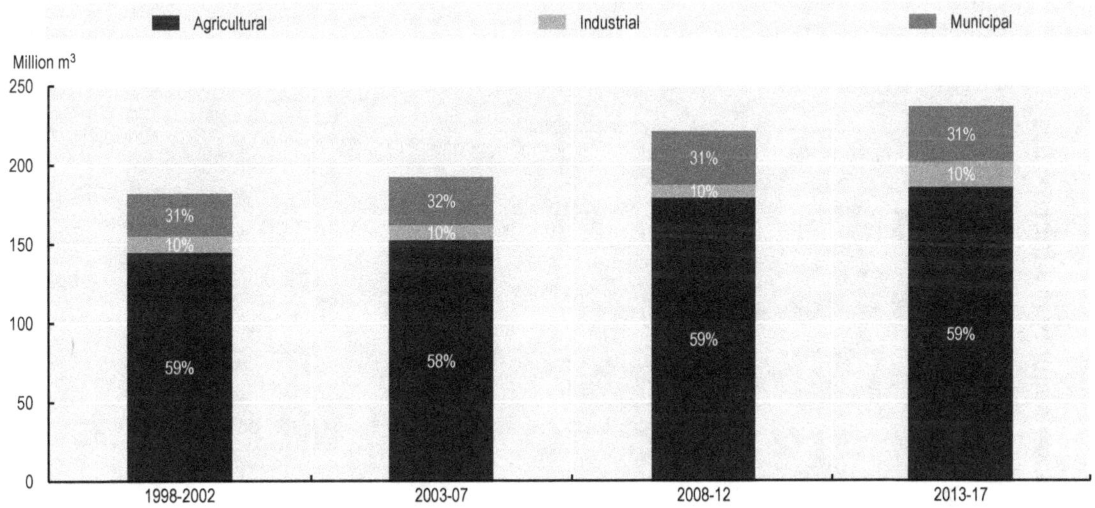

Source: FAO, (2021[53]), Aquastat database.

When asked about the most influential megatrends at the local level, respondent African cities to the OECD Survey on Water Governance (Annexes A and B) declare that climate, urbanisation and demographic changes, are on the megatrends that mostly affect water security (Table 1.7). Other megatrends also affect water resources and services, such as poverty alleviation, economic growth and food insecurity, although to a lesser extent.

Table 1.7. Key megatrends affecting water security in African cities

Cities	Climate change	Urbanisation	Demographic changes	Fighting poverty and inequalities	Economic development and growth	Food insecurity	Fighting water-borne diseases	Institutional and territorial reforms	Global crises
Brazzaville (Republic of the Congo)									
Lusaka (Zambia)									
Cocody (Cote d'Ivoire)									
Cotonou (Benin)									
Bangui (Central African Republic)									
Nouakchott (Mauritania)									
Saint-Louis (Senegal)									
Cape Town (South Africa)									
Monrovia (Liberia)									
Bangangte (Cameroon)									
Kampala (Uganda)									
Bama (Burkina Faso)									
Rosso (Mauritania)									
Accra (Ghana)									
Al Hoceima (Morocco)									
Fes (Morocco)									
Golf 3 (Togo)									
Tetouan (Morocco)									
Maputo (Mozambique)									
Kanembakache (Niger)									
Marrakech (Morocco)									

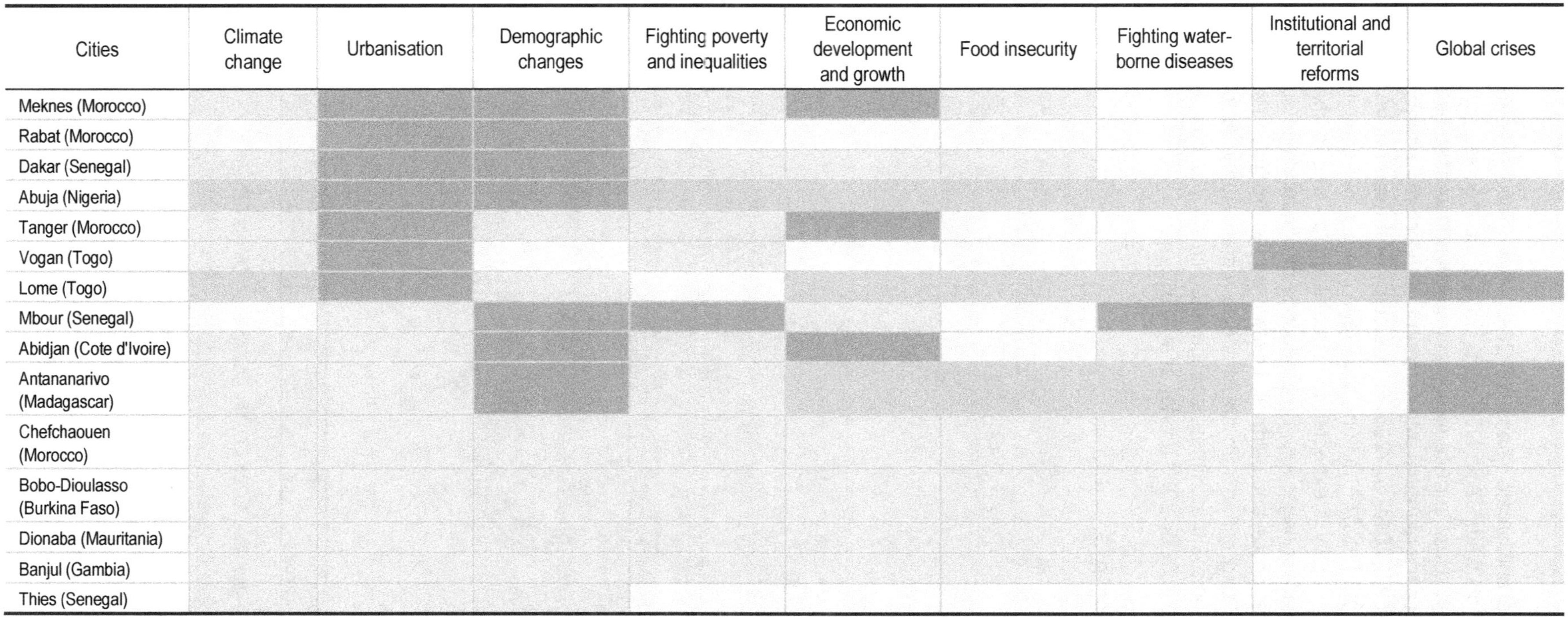

Cities	Climate change	Urbanisation	Demographic changes	Fighting poverty and inequalities	Economic development and growth	Food insecurity	Fighting water-borne diseases	Institutional and territorial reforms	Global crises
Meknes (Morocco)									
Rabat (Morocco)									
Dakar (Senegal)									
Abuja (Nigeria)									
Tanger (Morocco)									
Vogan (Togo)									
Lome (Togo)									
Mbour (Senegal)									
Abidjan (Cote d'Ivoire)									
Antananarivo (Madagascar)									
Chefchaouen (Morocco)									
Bobo-Dioulasso (Burkina Faso)									
Dionaba (Mauritania)									
Banjul (Gambia)									
Thies (Senegal)									

Note: 36 cities responded to the question "Which megatrends are putting water at risk in your city?".

Very important

Important

Not important

No answer

Source: OECD (2021[9]), *OECD Survey on Water Governance in African Cities*, OECD, Paris.

Climate change

According to the Intergovernmental Panel on Climate Change (IPCC), Africa is among the most vulnerable continents to climate change, which affects water security in many ways since the vast majority of climate change impact is felt in the water sector. "Near surface temperatures have increased by 0.5°C or more during the last 50 to 100 years over most parts of Africa, with minimum temperatures warming more rapidly than maximum temperatures" (Niang et al., 2014, p. 1206[46]). Projected temperatures in Africa will rise faster than the global average throughout the 21st century, thus reinforcing water scarcity and drought risks. Pressure on already limited water supply is expected to increase sharply due to changes in water cycles caused by erratic rainfall and to affect negatively the production of annual crops such as cereals and cotton, or perennial crops like coffee, cocoa and palm oil. This will lead to production shocks that will worsen food insecurity. Livestock may also suffer from the shrinking water supply, as grazing land is divided and damaged. Researchers estimate that climate change and climate hazards (Figure 1.5) will depress growth in global yields by 5% to 30% by 2050 (Porter et al., 2013[54]).

Figure 1.5. Climate hazards in Africa, 2016

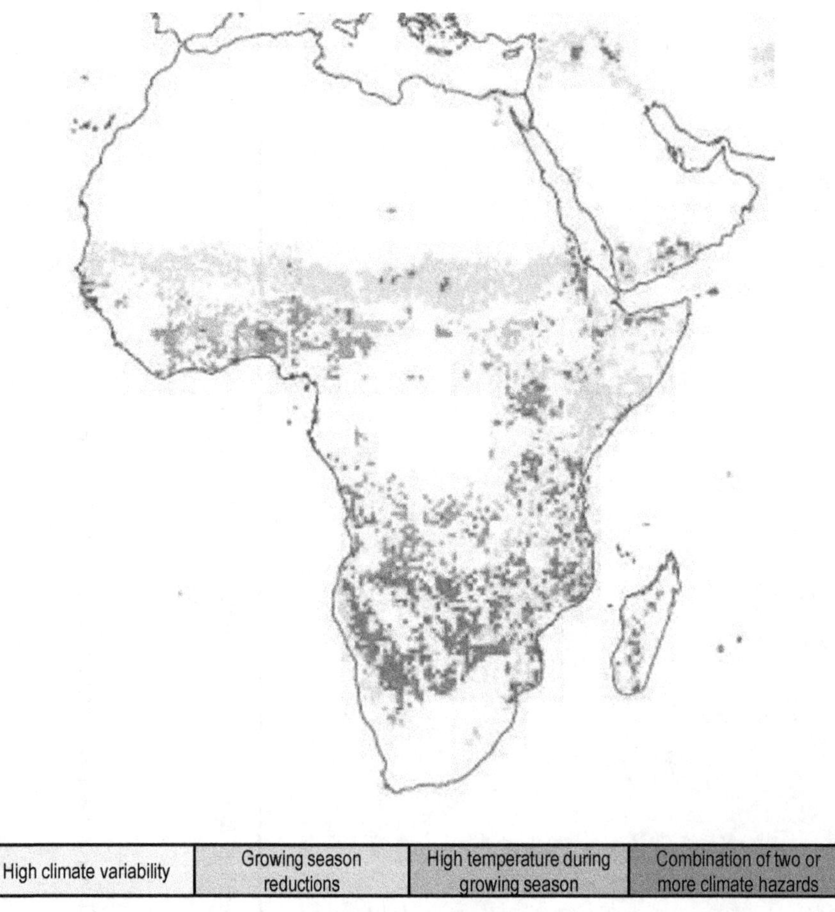

High climate variability	Growing season reductions	High temperature during growing season	Combination of two or more climate hazards

Source: Global Commission on Adaptation (2019[55]), *Adapt Now: A Global Call for Leadership on Climate Resilience.*

The Climate Change Vulnerability Index (CCVI),[1] which assesses the capacity of cities to withstand climate shocks, shows that two-thirds of African cities are at "extreme" risk, due to rising populations and poor urban infrastructure. The vulnerability is also driven by various factors including weak adaptive capacity, high dependence on ecosystem goods for livelihoods and less developed agricultural production systems. For instance, the city of Kinshasa, Democratic Republic of the Congo, which counts 13 million inhabitants, is exposed to weather shocks, including flooding, as well as droughts in surrounding areas, which could drag poor farmers into the city while disrupting water and food supplies. Along with other African cities, Kinshasa remains at high risk with cumulating factors of high poverty rates, expanding slums, weak governance and limited capacity to adapt to climate change. Its increasing urban population which is expected to double by 2035, will very likely intensify the city's already alarming risk profile in terms of access to drinking water or habitat. Among other cities most at risk of climate change are: Kampala, Uganda, where the annual population is set to grow by 5.1% a year on average between 2018-35; Dar-es-Salaam in Tanzania (4.8%); Abuja (4.5%) and Lagos (3.5%) in Nigeria; Addis Ababa (4.3%) in Ethiopia; and Luanda (3.7%) in Angola.

Urbanisation

Africapolis data highlight the staggering pace of the ongoing urbanisation transformation in Africa. Fifty percent of Africa's population live in one of the continent's 7 617 urban agglomerations. In 9 countries, the level of urbanisation is above 66% and a further 30 countries have an intermediary level of urbanisation between 33% and 65%. In 1950, only 4 countries had a level of urbanisation above 33%, while 35 countries were below 10%. North Africa is the continent's most urbanised region (78%), and Egypt and Libya the 2 countries with the highest levels of urbanisation with 93% and 81% respectively (Figure 1.6). The other 2 countries with a level of urbanisation above 80% are Gabon (81%) and São Tomé and Príncipe (80%). The countries with the lowest levels are Niger (17%), Burundi (21%), Eritrea (24%), Lesotho (26%) and South Sudan (27%).

Overall, countries with higher income levels in the African continent tend to have higher urbanisation levels. The only two low-income countries (gross national income per capita) with a level of urbanisation above 50% are Rwanda, with the highest population density, and Gambia, one of the smallest land areas. Similarly, the countries with the highest levels of urbanisation, Djibouti, Egypt, Gabon and Libya, are all middle-income countries and countries whose land areas are almost entirely desertic or with large forest areas, like Gabon. In these countries, the share of the agricultural population – the main activity of the rural population – is rather low.

Urbanisation dynamics are influenced by a variety of structural and socio-economic factors, such as geography and climate, population growth, size and density, income levels and economic structure, policies and institutions and cyclical factors such as environmental disasters, conflict and economic cycles. These factors are not of equal importance and vary over time depending on country contexts and interrelations. Since the 1990s, the major driver of urbanisation has been high population growth which contributes directly to the natural increase of urban populations.

This urban population growth in Africa is mostly absorbed by the outward expansion of metropolitan areas and secondary cities. As such, African cities are sprawling extensively, which exacerbates the spatial concentration of economic, environmental and social problems (World Resources Institute, 2019[47]) and holds significant implications for water supply and demand. Between now and 2050, two thirds of the urbanisation will happen in towns and intermediary cities (AfDB/OECD/UNDP, 2016[56]), which have less capacities to deploy infrastructure than larger cities. Because of this urban expansion pattern, African cities suffer from a lack of adequate formal housing and access to basic local public services, both in the informal settlements of the urban centre but also in the periphery. Indeed, densely populated informal settlements lack proper urban infrastructure. In most African cities, population and economic density is higher near the city centre and falls by 7% one kilometre away from the city centre, compared to 4% on average in other cities around the world. Night light intensity also falls by 15%, compared with 11% in cities elsewhere (Vinay, 2017[29]). This development pattern already poses many challenges in terms of planning, housing and basic infrastructure, and public services provision, among others. This is reflected in the heterogeneous development of planned and unplanned urban areas, the latter comprising informal settlements and peri-urban areas falling outside of the formal urban boundary and having rural and urban characteristics (Owusu, Agyei-Mensah and Lund, 2008[57]).

Urban growth in sub-Saharan African cities occurs predominantly in unplanned and informal settlements: 56% of urban dwellers in Africa live in these areas, compared to one-third in developing countries in general (UN, 2015[5]). Despite a slight decline of urban population living in slums over the past three decades, in some capital cities, informal settlements absorb the largest share of urban growth (Figure 1.7).

Figure 1.6. Change in the level of urbanisation in Africa from 1990 to 2015, as a percentage

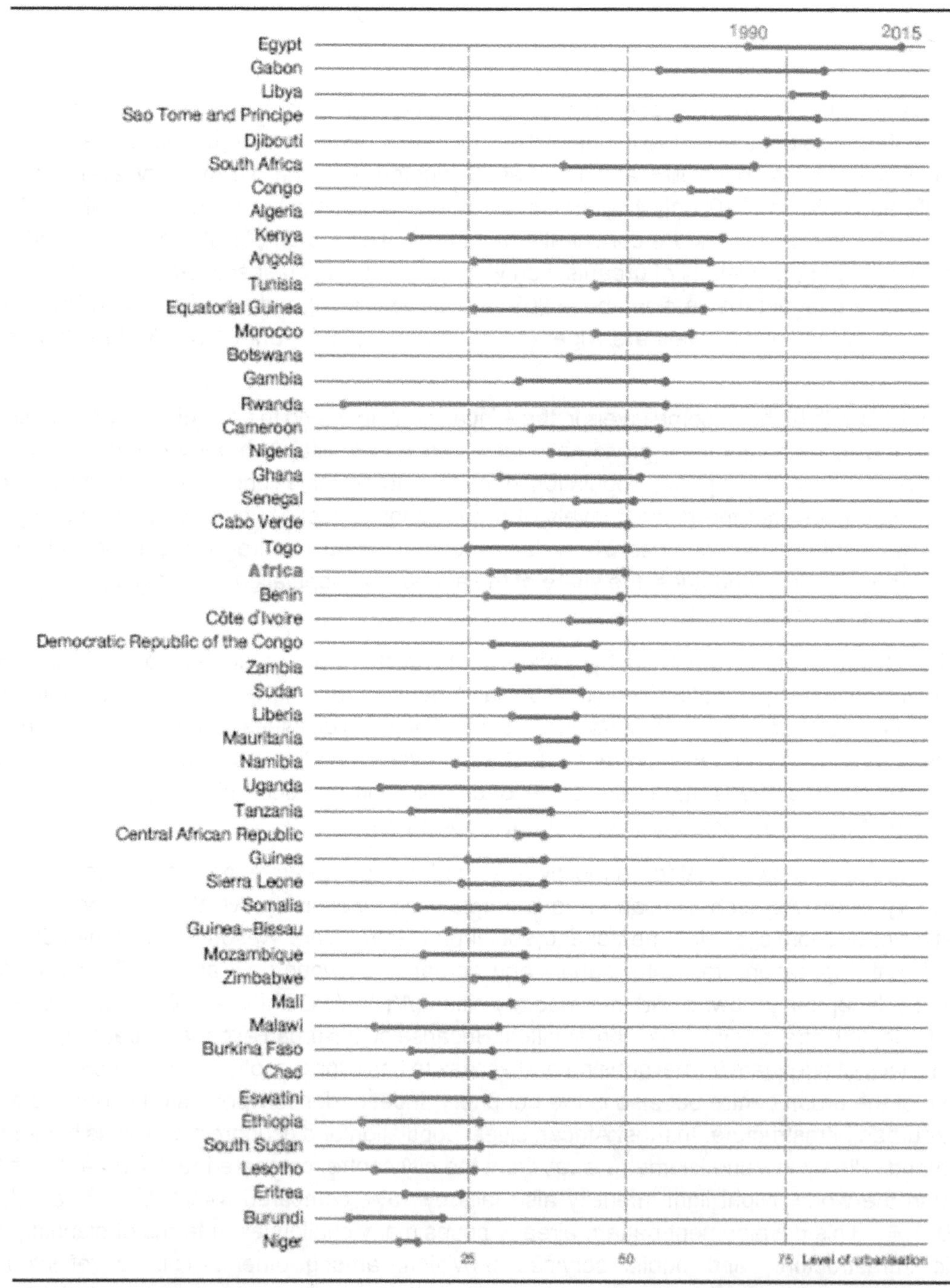

Source: OECD/SWAC 2018, Africapolis (database); Geopolis 2018Note: level of urbanisation expressed as a percentage; for instance, for Africa, the level of urbanisation increased from 31% in 1990 to 50% in 2015

Figure 1.7. Evolution of the share of urban population living slums in African countries, 1990-2018

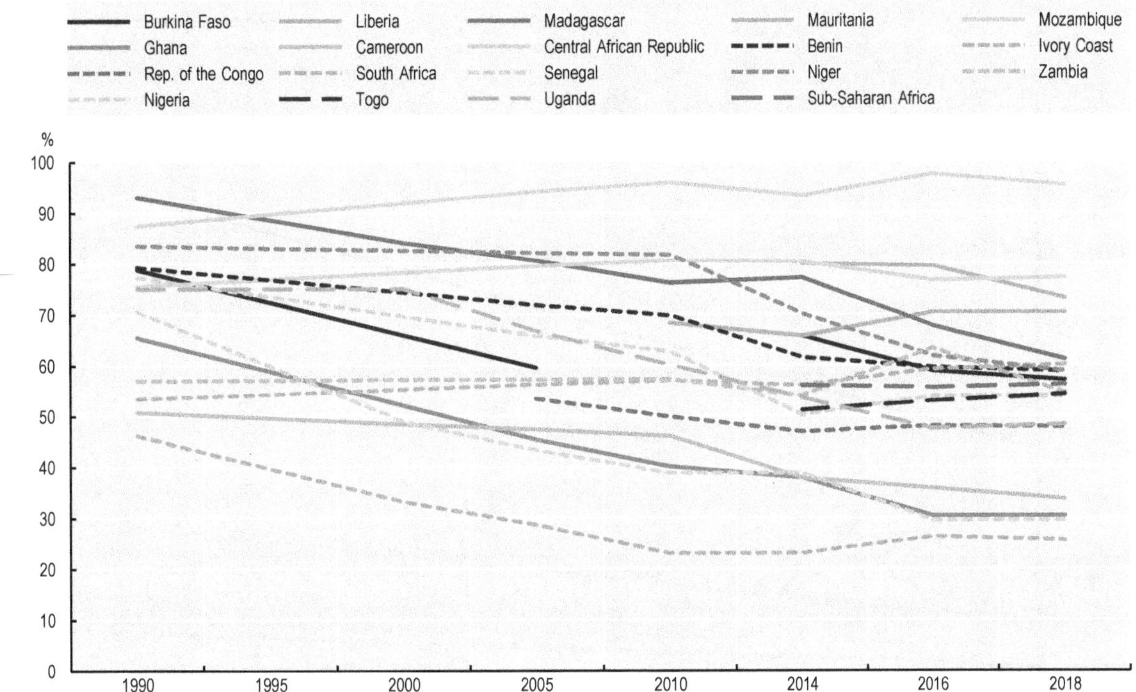

Source: UN-Habitat (2020[58]), *Urban Indicators Database*.

Unmanaged urban land expansion and sprawling, which are primarily driven by population growth, also have adverse effects on land use and the environment. Increasing conversion of surrounding agricultural land and water bodies has strong impacts on food production, habitats and biodiversity conservation. Increased urban sprawl also means increased greenhouse gas emissions, air pollution and urban heat. Recent projections foresee that in mid-latitudinal Africa, urban areas are expected to increase by nearly 20-fold by 2030 compared with a 2000 baseline, with the largest forecasted increase in the vicinity of environmentally protected areas (Güneralp et al., 2017[59]).

Demographic change

For the past decades, Africa has witnessed a dramatic demographic increase, which is expected to continue in the future. The total population of Africa rose from 177 million in 1950 to more than 1.34 billion in 2020 (Worldometer (n.d.[60]), based on UN estimates) which represents 16.2% of the world's population. Despite a decline in fertility rates in most sub-Saharan African countries, which still remain the highest in the world, the population is expected to reach more than 2 billion by 2050 (UN, 2015[5]). The projected population by 2050 in Africa shows disparities among African regions. Eastern, Western and Central Africa population is expected to more than double while Northern and Southern Africa population will increase to a lesser extent (Figure 1.8).

The overall population increase in Africa was more concentrated in cities. In 2015, more than 560 million Africans lived in one of the continent's 7 617 urban agglomerations compared to only 27 million in 1950 (Figure 1.9). When focusing on sub-Saharan African only, the urban population is projected to more than triple from 346 million to 1.1 billion by 2050 (UN, 2015[5]). Thus, urban sub-Saharan African population is estimated to grow from 41% in 2019 to 60% in 2050 (UN, 2015[5]).

Figure 1.8. Projected total population by 2050 of Africa and African regions

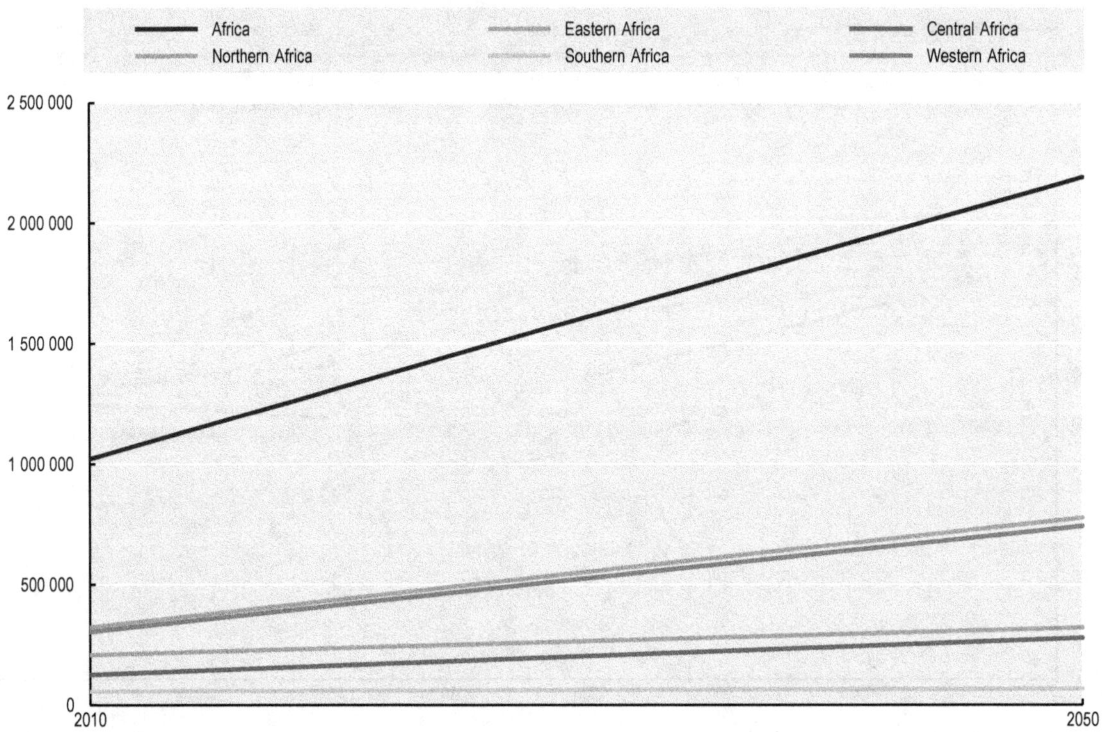

Source: UN (2015[5]), *World Urbanization Prospects: The 2014 Revision*, ST/ESA/SER.A/366, Population Division, Department of Economic and Social Affairs, United Nations.

Figure 1.9. Evolution of Urban population in Africa, 1950-2015

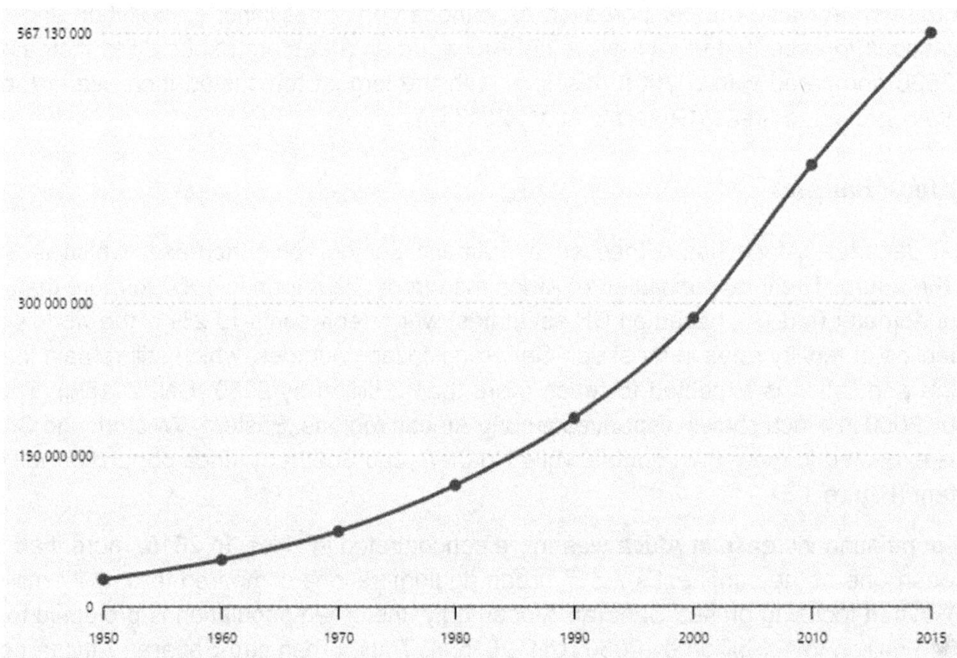

Source: OECD (n.d.[61]), *An Unprecedented Pace of Urbanisation – Africa*, http://www.oecd.org/africa-urbanisation/#discover-data.

The period between 1950 and 1980 saw the fastest urban growth with Africa's urban population increasing 5.1% annually. Especially in the least urbanised regions of Central Africa, East Africa and West Africa this period was marked by very high urban growth rates, averaging between 6.4% and 8%. Between 1980 and 2000, urban growth decelerated to 4.4% for Africa as a whole and increased again to 4.7% for the period 2000-15. With a current average annual growth rate above 4%, 86 of the 100 fastest-growing cities in the world are located in Africa. Sub-Saharan African's cities have grown at an average rate of 4% per year over the past 20 years, and are projected to grow between 3% and 4% annually from 2015 to 2055. In comparison, globally the average annual urban population growth rate is projected to range from 1.44% to 1.84% from 2015 to 2030 (WHO 2015) (Figure 1.10).

Figure 1.10. Annual evolution and projection of urban population growth rate, 1950-2050

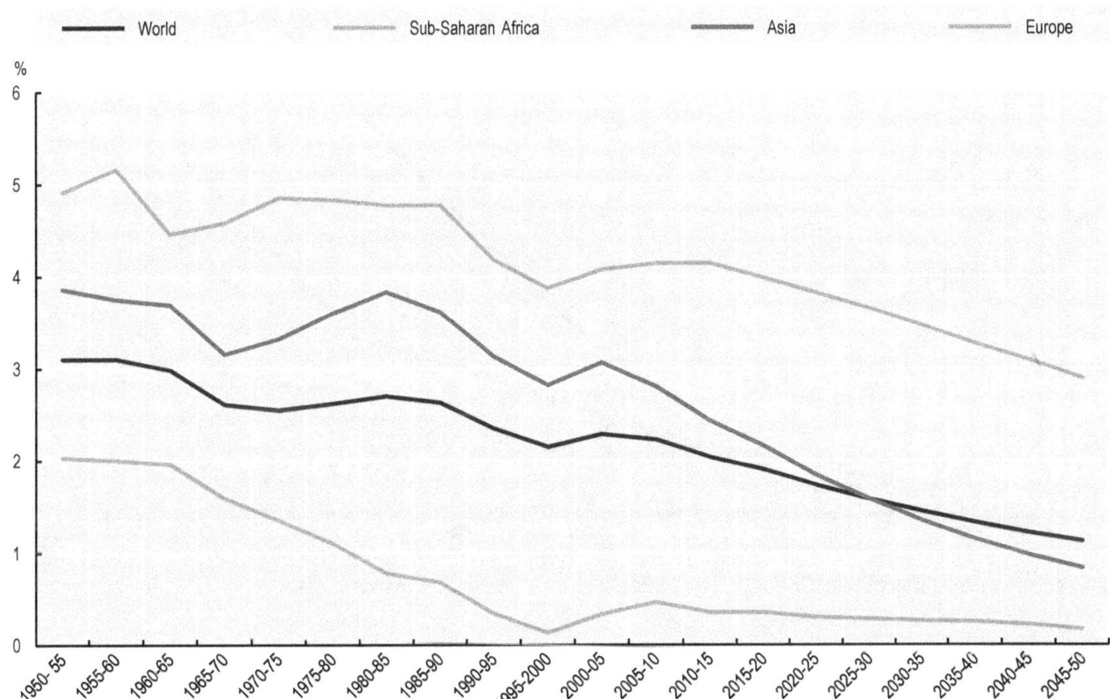

Source: (UN, 2015[5]).

Participating African cities in the OECD Survey on Water Governance are no exception to this rapid population growth, with annual rates ranging from 2% to more than 20% over the past decade (Figure 1.11).

Although the rapid urban population increase is mainly caused by the high rate of natural increase in towns and the re-classification of hinterland settlements into urban areas, intra-regional migration also accounts for a significant proportion of urban population growth in Africa. Since 1990, African migration was predominantly intra-continental, although the distribution and migration routes changed over time. In 2000, the stock of international migrants originating from Africa and living in Africa was the main stock amounting to 12.5 million persons, highlighting that migration was foremost an intra-African phenomenon. This stock grew consistently to reach 19.4 million in 2017 (UNCTAD, 2018[62]) This intra-continental migration is significantly affecting water security as most migrants settle in urban areas, thus increasing water demand and putting further pressure on water and sanitation infrastructure.

Figure 1.11. Population growth in select African cities, 1950-2015

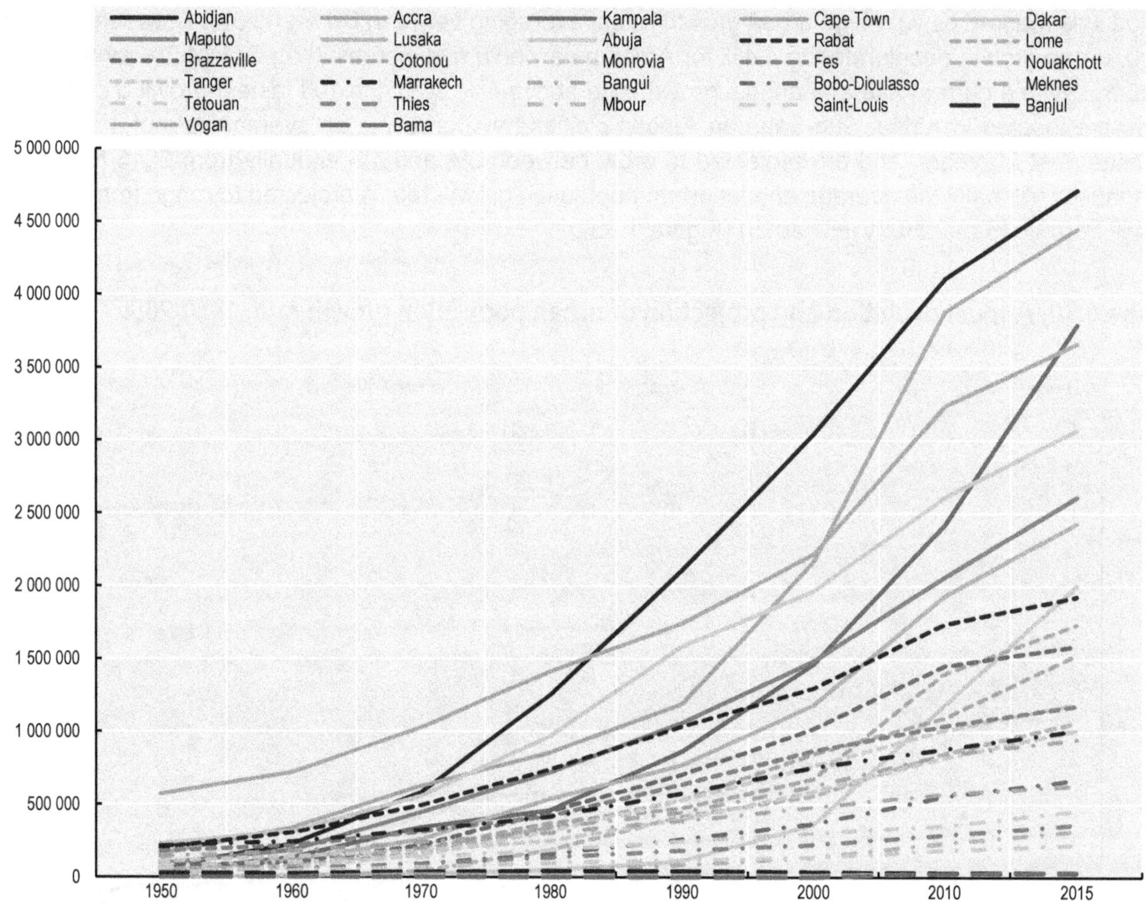

Source: Selection of responding cities to OECD (2021[9]), *OECD Survey on Water Governance in African Cities*, OECD, Paris; with data from Africapolis (n.d.[63]), *Homepage*, https://africapolis.org/home.

COVID-19 and water security in African cities

As in many cities around the world, COVID-19 has acted as a magnifying glass on pressing water challenges, stressing and widening amongst others existing inequalities in access to water and sanitation services. Handwashing is one of the top preventive measures recommended to reduce the spread of COVID-19. However, current levels of handwashing with soap are generally low across the African continent. Monitoring handwashing behaviour is difficult but the presence of soap and water at a designated place is generally used as a proxy indicator. According to UNICEF data from 2017, the majority of Sahelian and West African people did not have basic handwashing facilities available at home. Only Ghana, Mali, Mauritania and Nigeria were above the global average of 60% of people with access to basic facilities. The situation was particularly worrisome in small countries such as Benin, Gambia, Guinea-Bissau, Liberia and Togo where at least three-quarters of the population had no handwashing facility at home. Nigeria is among the countries with the largest number of people with no access to a handwashing facility in the world (49 million), following Indonesia (78 million) and the Democratic Republic of the Congo (69 million). In urban areas in Africa, 55% of the population has access to basic sanitation services (i.e. improved sanitation facilities not shared with other households) and 47% has basic handwashing facilities at home (UN-Habitat, 2020[64]). These shares descend to 44% and 37% respectively for urban areas in sub-Saharan Africa. There are significant gaps between the richest and poorest within a country.

While rural areas are generally less well-equipped than urban areas in terms of handwashing facilities, urban populations are particularly at risk of COVID-19 contamination considering the higher population density and the large number of crowded places such as markets or public transport. In fact, over 95% of confirmed COVID-19 cases worldwide are in urban areas (UN-Habitat, 2020[64]). Public handwashing facilities are generally rare and often lack soap in African urban areas. Mobile handwashing facilities are very common in Western Africa (Figure 1.12), for example, the use of jugs or basins to wash hands before and after meals. However, mobile facilities often lack soap and sufficient water. Beyond contributing to contain the COVID-19 pandemic, washing hands is also a basic preventive measure, which can help eradicate many other communicable diseases such as cholera, which is still prevalent in the region.

Figure 1.12. Fixed versus mobile handwashing facilities in select African countries

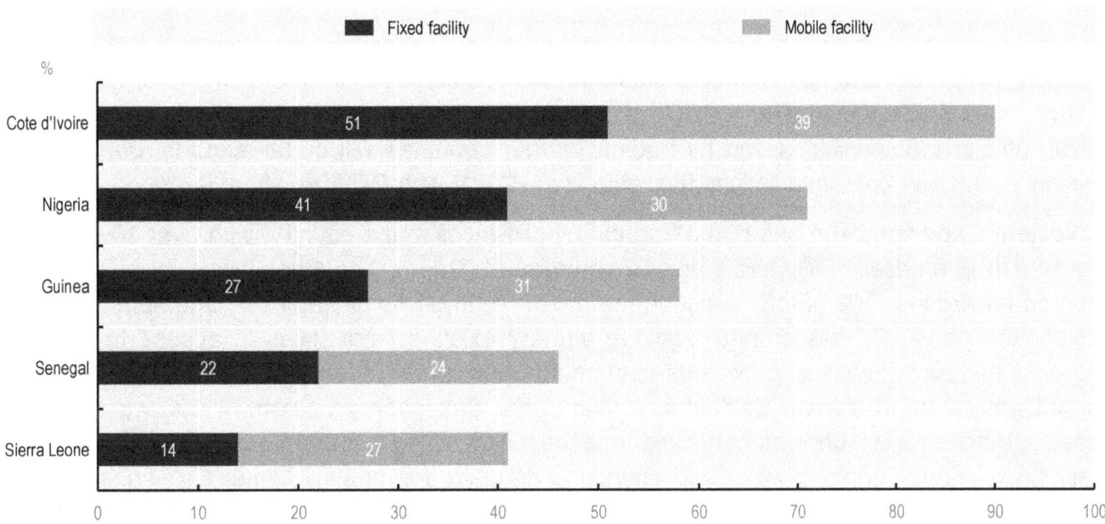

Source: UNICEF/WHO (2019[65]), "Progress on household drinking water, sanitation and hygiene (2000-2017), special focus on inequalities".

In the medium term, the loss of public revenue due to the contraction of economic activity could potentially limit government investment in water and sanitation. In 2020, GDP was estimated to fall by -1% in North Africa[2] and by -3.2% in sub-Saharan Africa (IMF, 2020[66]; 2020[67]). The economic slowdown has negatively affected public revenue in most sub-Saharan African countries, especially oil-exporting economies, but grants are projected to increase revenues in a few countries (Burkina Faso, Chad, Niger and Senegal). Many national governments in Africa took measures to ensure adequate water supply in response to the pandemic, with policy responses ranging from short-term subsidies or exemptions from paying water bills to more long-term plans to improve water supply and access to water and sanitation facilities. In some cases, however, both public and private longer-term investments may have been delayed or cancelled due to loss of public revenue and the economic situation.

In South Africa, while COVID-19 has hit the Western Cape Province particularly hard with 270 691 cases and 10 731 deaths (20% of total deaths in South Africa), located essentially in the city of Cape Town, the city administration has shown remarkable resilience in dealing with the pandemic, drawing extensively on lessons from past crises such as droughts (Box 1.4).

Box 1.4. How Cape Town Water Crisis paved the way for COVID-19 crisis management

Covid-19 impacts on South Africa and Cape Town

Like most other countries around the globe, South Africa has been hit hard by the COVID-19 pandemic, with over 1 485 000 confirmed cases of COVID-19 and over 47 400 deaths (as of February 2021) (WHO, 2021[68]). Though the impact of the pandemic has been relatively mitigated on the African continent in relation to other regions, South Africa has the continent's highest caseload as of March 2021 and continues to bear the highest burden of the pandemic, with 69% of total deaths (as of January 2021) and 57% of all reported and confirmed cases in the African region (WHO, 2021[69]). In addition to human casualties, the COVID-19 pandemic and the ensuing lockdown have triggered a sharp drop in economic activity.

South Africa reacted quickly to the outbreak by establishing a nationwide lockdown on 26 March 2020. Economic activity was reduced in mining and industry, and stopped in the tourism, entertainment and passenger transport sectors. The OECD (2020[70]) estimates that in a double-hit scenario, a new outbreak affecting South Africa and its trading partner countries will curtail exports, deepening the recession to -8.2% in 2020 and limiting the recovery in 2021, with GDP growth at 0.6%.

The Western Cape has been one of the hardest-hit provinces in the country, with over 10 000 deaths and over 270 000 cases (Western Cape Government, 2020[71]). The Cape Town metropolitan area accounted for around 70% of total cases in the province. In terms of water management and service provision, the pandemic has emphasised the already existing inequalities in access to water and sanitation services in townships, informal settlements and among the homeless in Cape Town. The national Department of Human Settlements, Water and Sanitation procured 41 000 water tanks for national distribution to ensure water supply during the lockdown so that people in these living conditions can still have enough drinking water and maintain adequate and healthy hygiene routines. However, there are very significant concerns about the spread of COVID-19 in informal settlements through communal toilets and taps, as well as security concerns around the use of water tanks (Hara, Ncube and Sibanda, 2020[72]).

COVID-19 poses many challenges to the water sector encompassing economic and social issues. A sustainable funding model for water and sanitation is needed but under so many stressed conditions and with tariffs set below cost-recovery level, it will be challenging to finance all of the necessary water investments to achieve resilience while addressing basic human and social needs. The National Water and Sanitation Plan, which sets outs the country's approach to address, among other issues, inequalities in access to water and sanitation for the poor in cities, will be tested through the pandemic, especially with regards to the co-ordination between funding capacity and funding needs, in light of the added pressure that the pandemic entails in terms of resources.

From crisis management to the "new normal"

Lessons learned during the critical stages of Cape Town's 2017-18 water crisis have helped the city cope with the hardships imposed by the pandemic in 2019-20.

In fact, terminology which has become used globally such as the "new normal", which makes a reference to the realisation that the crisis brought on by the pandemic will bring about permanent change, was already used by stakeholders in the Western Cape to reference the effects of the drought and the predicted impacts of climate change. Like the drought, the pandemic has precipitated changes that had profound economic impacts, with direct losses in earnings at many levels experienced by individuals, as well as countries' GDP and growth rates. In addition, social changes in the way people live and work have been brought about. Furthermore, the environmental aspect of both crises is undeniable, with the longer-term impacts of climate change becoming more and more visible.

Some important lessons learned during the drought shaped the city's response to COVID-19. For example, both crises led the Western Cape Government and Cape Town to value the importance of effective communication with citizens and stakeholders for co-ordinated action and trust-building. This need for collaborative and open interactions between stakeholders has also become apparent during the COVID-19 crisis, where, despite the difficult conditions, municipal stakeholders have worked together through transversal committees to minimise the impact of COVID-19 on its residents in a more cohesive way, a method that was put into practice with the water crisis.

COVID-19 may provide the impulse necessary towards a green recovery, building off the 2019 Cape Town Resilience Strategy implemented as a response to the water crisis. For example, the impulse to prioritise investment in ecosystem services such as the clearing of alien invasive species as a more cost-effective way to augment water supply may become stronger now, in times of funding limitations brought about by the pandemic. However, the full impact of COVID-19 is yet to be seen and the future remains uncertain as long as the pandemic remains rampant.

Source: Author's elaboration based on Hara, M., B. Ncube and D. Sibanda (2020[72]), "Water and sanitation in the face of Covid-19 in Cape Town's townships and informal settlements"; OECD (2020[70]), *OECD Economic Surveys: South Africa 2020*, https://doi.org/10.1787/530e7ce0-en; Western Cape Government (2020[71]), *Covid-19 Dashboard*, Covid-19 Response; WHO (2021[68]), *South Africa: WHO Coronavirus Disease (COVID-19) Dashboard*, World Health Organization; WHO (2021[69]), *COVID-19 Situation Update for the WHO Africa Region*, World Health Organization.

References

ActionAid (2006), *Climate Change, Urban Flooding and the Rights of the Urban Poor in Africa: Key Findings from Six African Cities*. [20]

AfDB/OECD/UNDP (2016), *African Economic Outlook 2016: Sustainable Cities and Structural Transformation*, OECD Publishing, Paris, https://dx.doi.org/10.1787/aeo-2016-en. [56]

Africapolis (n.d.), *Homepage*, https://africapolis.org/home. [63]

Awuor, C., V. Orindi and A. Adwera (2008), "Climate change and coastal cities: The case of Mombasa, Kenya", *Environment and Urbanization*, Vol. 20/1, pp. 231–242. [49]

Barros, V. et al. (eds.) (2014), *Africa*, Cambridge University Press. [46]

Begum, S., M. Stive and J. Hall (eds.) (2007), *Flood Risk Management in Europe: Innovation in Policy and Practice*, Springer Science. [15]

City of Cape Town (2020), *City of Cape Town Website*. [32]

Climat, environnement, société (2012), "Conference on "Water Scarcity in Africa: Issues and Challenges"", 3 October 2012, Paris, France, https://web.archive.org/web/20160327004419/http://gisclimat.fr/en/node/1417. [45]

Douglas (2017), "Flooding in African cities, scales of causes, teleconnections, risks, vulnerability and impacts", *International Journal of Disaster Risk Reduction*, Vol. 26, http://dx.doi.org/10.1016/j.ijdrr.2017.09.024. [13]

Douglas, I. et al. (2008), "Unjust waters: Climate change, flooding and the urban poor in Africa", *Environment and Urbanization*, Vol. 20/1, pp. 187–205. [22]

EM-DAT (2020), *EM-DAT Database*, https://www.emdat.be/database. [10]

Etuonovbe, A. (2011), "The devastating effect of flooding in Nigeria", FIG Working Week, Bridging the Gap between Cultures, Marrakech, Morocco, 18-22 May. [19]

FAO (2021), *AquaStat*, http://www.fao.org/aquastat/en/. [53]

Garrick, D. et al. (2019), *Informal Water Markets in an Urbanising World: Some Unanswered Questions*, World Bank, Washington, DC. [38]

Global Commission on Adaptation (2019), *Adapt Now: A Global Call for Leadership on Climate Resilience*. [55]

Güneralp, B. et al. (2017), "Urbanization in Africa: Challenges and opportunities for conservation", *Environmental Research Letter*, Vol. 13/015002. [59]

Guzmán, D. and J. Stoler (2018), "An evolving choice in a diverse water market: A quality comparison of sachet water with community and household water sources in Ghana", *American Journal of Tropical Medicine and Hygiene*, Vol. 99/2. [41]

Hallegatte, S. et al. (2013), "Future flood losses in major coastal cities", *Nature Climate Change*, Vol. 3, pp. 802-806. [11]

Hara, M., B. Ncube and D. Sibanda (2020), "Water and sanitation in the face of Covid-19 in Cape Town's townships and informal settlements". [72]

Hawkins (2017), *The impacts of bottled water: an analysis of bottled water markets and their interactions with tap water provision*. [35]

Housing Development Agency, South Africa (2014), *Informal settlements: Rapid assessment and categorisation*, https://www.pptrust.org.za/wp-content/uploads/delightful-downloads/rapid-assessment-and-categorisation-guidelines-2014.pdf. [31]

Houston, D. et al. (2011), "Pluvial (rain-related) flooding in urban areas: The invisible hazard", Joseph Rowntree Foundation, New York. [16]

IMF (2020), *Regional Economic Outlook: Middle East and Central Asia*, International Monetary Fund, Washington, DC. [66]

IMF (2020), *Regional Economic Outlook: Sub-Saharan Africa*, International Monetary Fund, Washington, DC, http://imf.org/-/media/Files/Publications/REO/AFR/2020/October/English/text.ashx. [67]

Kariuki, S. (2005), *Small Scale Private Service Providers of Water Supply and Electricity: A Review of Incidence, Structure, Pricing and Operating Characteristics*. [34]

Kinuthia-Njenga, B. (2009), *Climate Change and Migration in Nairobi*, Report prepared for the World Bank. [48]

Lall, S., J. Henderson and A. Venables (2017), *Africa's Cities: Opening Doors to the World*, World Bank, Washington, DC. [26]

McDonald, R. et al. (2011), "Urban growth, climate change, and freshwater availability", *PNAS*, Vol. 108/15, pp. 6312-6317, https://doi.org/10.1073/pnas.1011615108. [28]

Merz, B., A. Thieken and M. Gocht (2007), "Flood risk mapping at the local scale: Concepts and challenges", in Begum, S., M. Stive and J. Hall (eds.), *Flood Risk Management in Europe: Innovation in Policy and Practice*, Springer, London. [17]

Nchito, W. (2007), "Flood risk in unplanned settlements in Lusaka", *Environment and Urbanization*, Vol. 19/2, pp. 539–551. [23]

Ndaruzaniye, V. et al. (2010), "Climate change and security in Africa: Vulnerability discussion paper", *Africa Climate Change Environment and Security*, Vol. 3/9. [7]

Nkwunonwo, U., M. Whitworth and B. Baily (2016), "A review and critical analysis of the efforts towards urban flood reduction in the Lagos region of Nigeria", *Natural Hazards and Earth System Science*, Vol. 16, pp. 349-369. [14]

OECD (2021), *OECD Survey on Water Governance in African Cities*, OECD, Paris. [9]

OECD (2020), *OECD Economic Surveys: South Africa 2020*, OECD Publishing, Paris, https://doi.org/10.1787/530e7ce0-en. [70]

OECD (2015), *OECD Principles on Water Governance*, OECD, Paris, https://www.oecd.org/gov/regional-policy/OECD-Principles-on-Water-Governancebrochure.pdf. [4]

OECD (2013), *Water Security for Better Lives*, OECD Studies on Water, OECD Publishing, Paris, http://dx.doi.org/10.1787/9789264202405-en. [2]

OECD (2012), *OECD Environmental Outlook 2050*, https://doi.org/10.1787/1999155x. [3]

OECD (n.d.), *An Unprecedented Pace of Urbanisation - Africa*, OECD, Paris, http://www.oecd.org/africa-urbanisation/#discover-data. [61]

OECD (forthcoming), *Water Governance in Cape Town*, OECD Publishing, Paris. [33]

Owusu, G., S. Agyei-Mensah and R. Lund (2008), "Slums of hope and slums of despair: Mobility and livelihoods in Nima, Accra", *Norsk Geografisk Tidsskrift – Norwegian Journal of Geography*, Vol. 62/3. [57]

Parks (2019), *Experiences and lessons in managing water from Cape Town*, Imperial College London. [52]

Pharoah, R. (2014), "Built-in risk: Linking housing concerns and flood risk in subsidized housing settlements in Cape Town, South Africa", *International Journal of Disaster Risk Science*, Vol. 5, pp. 313–322. [25]

Porter, J. et al. (2013), "Food security and food production systems", in *Turn Down the Heat: Climate Extremes, Regional Impacts, and the Case for Resilience*, World Bank, Washington, DC. [54]

Satterthwaite (2008), *Towards Pro-Poor Adaptation to Climate Change in the Urban Centres of Low- and Middle- Income Countries*, The Global Urban Research Centre, p. 44. [21]

Sawadogo, D. (2015), "Delivering city-wide WASH services: reaching informal settlements in Ouagadougou, Burkina Faso". [39]

SDGC/A and SDSN (2020), *Africa SDG Index and Dashboards Report 2020*, Sustainable Development Goals Center for Africa and Sustainable Development Solutions Network. [8]

Simatele, M., J. Binns and M. Simatele (2012), "Sustaining livelihoods under a changing climate: The case of urban agriculture in Lusaka, Zambia", *Journal of Environmental Planning and Management*, Vol. 55/9, pp. 1175–1191. [50]

Solo (2003), *Independent Water Entrepreneurs in Latin America: The other private sector in water services.*. [37]

Tiepolo, M. (2014), "Flood risk reduction and climate change in large cities south of the Sahara", in Macchi, S. and M. Tiepolo (eds.), *Climate Change Vulnerability in Southern African Cities*, Springer, Switzerland. [12]

UN (2015), *World Urbanization Prospects: The 2014 Revision*, ST/ESA/SER.A/366, Population Division, Department of Economic and Social Affairs, United Nations. [5]

UN (2014), *Water for Life - Africa*, United Nations, https://www.un.org/waterforlifedecade/africa.shtml#:~:text=About%2066%25%20of%20Africa%20is,poor%20hygiene%20and%20contaminated%20water. [44]

UNCTAD (2018), *Economic Development in Africa Report 2018.* [62]

UN-Habitat (2020), *UN-Habitat COVID-19 Response Plan*, http://unhabitat.org/sites/default/files/2020/04/final_un-habitat_covid-19_response_plan.pdf. [64]

UN-Habitat (2020), *Urban Indicators Database.* [58]

UNICEF/WHO (2019), "Progress on household drinking water, sanitation and hygiene (2000-2017), special focus on inequalities", United Nations Children's Fund and World Health Organization. [65]

UN-Water (n.d.), *Indicator 6.3.1 – Wastewater Treatment*, https://www.sdg6data.org/indicator/6.3.1. [42]

UN-Water (n.d.), *Indicator 6.3.2 – Water Quality*, https://www.sdg6data.org/indicator/6.3.2. [43]

USAID (2015), *Sustainable Water and Sanitation for Africa: Final Report*, United States Agency for International Development. [40]

Verisk, Maplecroft (2018), *Climate Change Vulnerability Index*, https://www.maplecroft.com/risk-indices/climate-change-vulnerability-index/. [6]

Viljoen, M. and H. Booysen (2006), "Planning and management of flood damage control: The South African experience", *Irrigation and Drainage*, Vol. 55/1, pp. S83–S91. [24]

Vinay, H. (2017), *Africa's Cities: Opening Doors to the World.* [29]

Vojinović (2015), *Flood Risk: The Holistic Perspective: From Integrated to Interactive Planning for Flood Resilience*, http://dx.doi.org/10.2166/9781780405339. [18]

Vörösmarty, C. et al. (2010), "Global threats to human water security and river biodiversity", *Nature and Resources*, Vol. 467, pp. 555-561. [30]

Western Cape Government (2020), *Covid-19 Dashboard*, Covid-19 Response. [71]

WHO (2021), *COVID-19 Situation Update for the WHO Africa Region*, World Health Organization. [69]

WHO (2021), *South Africa: WHO Coronavirus Disease (COVID-19) Dashboard*, World Health Organization. [68]

WHO/UNICEF (2019), "Progress on household drinking water, sanitation and hygiene 2000-17. Special focus on inequalities", World Health Organization and United Nations Children's Fund, New York. [27]

World Economic Forum (2020), *World Economic Forum's Global Risks Report*. [1]

World Resources Institute (2019), *Upward and Outward Growth: Managing Urban Expansion for More Equitable Cities in the Global South*. [47]

World Wildlife Fund (2018), *Agricultural water file: Farming for a drier future*, https://www.wwf.org.za/water/?25441/Agricultural-water-file-Farming-for-a-drier-future. [51]

Worldometer (n.d.), *Africa Population*, https://www.worldometers.info/world-population/africa-population/. [60]

Wutich, B. (2016), *Can Informal Water Vendors Deliver on the Promise of A Human Right to Water? Results From Cochabamba, Bolivia*, pp. 14-24. [36]

Notes

[1] The term informal suppliers refers to all types of water suppliers who are not operating in the legal framework of water management in an area. It refers to any form of non-utility water service and it includes all small-scale entrepreneurs that are institutionally and contractually independent of the utility. "Informal" is related both to the technical systems of provision (which may include the infrastructure and the sale of water) and the resulting relationships (Misra, K. 2014. From formal-informal to emergent formalisation: Fluidities in the production of urban waterscapes. Water Alternatives 7(1): 15-34).

[1] The 2018 Climate Change Vulnerability Index uses some 50 existing data, ranging from climate models to economic factors, including demographic projections, to assess the vulnerability of humans to climate change and extreme weather events within a thirty-year timeframe (Verisk, Maplecroft, 2018[6]).

[2] In IMF (2020[66]), the closest proxy to North African countries is the IMF's Middle East, North Africa, Afghanistan and Pakistan (MENAP) region, focusing on countries that are oil importers as opposed to oil exporters (MENAP oil importers). This group of countries consists of Afghanistan, Djibouti, Egypt, Jordan, Lebanon, Mauritania, Morocco, Pakistan, Somalia, Sudan, Syria, Tunisia, and West Bank and Gaza Strip.

2 Mapping key water policies and institutions in African cities

This chapter assesses the state of play of water policies and institutions in African countries and cities. It does so by describing who does what at the national and city levels. It thus underlines the complexity of water resources and services policy and management in Africa.

Coping with current and future water challenges requires robust public policies, targeting measurable objectives in predetermined time schedules at the appropriate scale, relying on a clear assignment of duties across responsible authorities and subject to regular monitoring and evaluation. Water governance can greatly contribute to the design and implementation of such policies, in a shared responsibility across levels of government, civil society, businesses and the broader range of stakeholders that have an important role to play alongside policymakers to reap the economic, social and environmental benefits of good water governance.

Assessing the state of play of water governance in African cities requires understanding who does what in water policy design and implementation. Providing such a mapping is the first step to clearly distinguishing key roles and responsibilities for policymaking, policy implementation, operational management, information, monitoring, regulation and financing. This chapter specifies who does what by assessing water-related policies and institutions at the national and city levels in Africa.

The mapping presented at the city level builds upon responses collected from a sample of 36 African cities to an OECD Survey on Water Governance carried out between May and September 2020 (Box 2.1).

Box 2.1. OECD Survey on Water Governance in African cities

Data were collected with the support of UCLG Africa from May to September 2020, for a total of 36 cities in Africa (Figure 2.1): Abidjan (Côte d'Ivoire); Abuja (Nigeria); Accra (Ghana); Al Hoceima (Morocco); Antananarivo (Madagascar); Bama (Burkina Faso); Bangangte (Cameroon); Bangui (Central African Republic); Banjul (Gambia); Bobo-Dioulasso (Burkina Faso); Brazzaville (Republic of the Congo); Cape Town (South Africa); Chefchaouen (Morocco); Cocody (Côte d'Ivoire); Cotonou (Benin); Dakar (Senegal); Dionaba (Mauritania); Fes (Morocco); Golf 3 (Togo); Kampala (Uganda); Kanembakache (Niger); Lome (Togo); Lusaka (Zambia); Maputo (Mozambique); Marrakech (Morocco); Mbour (Senegal); Meknes (Morocco); Monrovia (Liberia); Nouakchott (Mauritania); Rabat (Morocco); Rosso (Mauritania); Saint-Louis (Senegal); Tanger (Morocco); Tetouan (Morocco); Thies (Senegal); and Vogan (Togo).

Figure 2.1. Respondent African cities to the OECD Survey on Water Governance

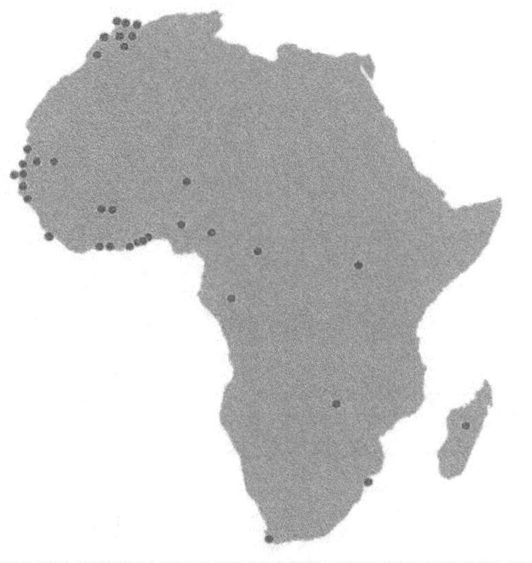

Source: OECD (2021[1]), *OECD Survey on Water Governance in African Cities*, OECD, Paris.

The cities surveyed comprise 15 capital cities (42% of the sample and 28% of total number of capital cities in Africa) and 77% of French-speaking African cities despite efforts to include cities from English- and Portuguese-speaking African countries to better balance the sample. Although the overall sample includes a balanced representation of cities of various sizes (Table 2.1), it is not representative in terms of the geographical scope.

Table 2.1. Participating African cities in the OECD Survey on Water Governance

Inhabitants	Share of cities in the sample (%)	Cities
> 3 million	25	Abidjan (Côte d'Ivoire), Abuja (Nigeria), Accra (Ghana), Antananarivo (Madagascar), Brazzaville (Republic of the Congo), Cape Town (South Africa), Dakar (Senegal), Kampala (Uganda), Lusaka (Zambia)
From 1 to 3 million	25	Bangui (Central African Republic), Cotonou (Benin), Fes (Morocco), Lome (Togo), Maputo (Mozambique), Monrovia (Liberia), Nouakchott (Mauritania), Rabat (Morocco), Tanger (Morocco)
From 300 000 to 1 million	22	Banjul (Gambie), Cocody (Côte d'Ivoire), Bobo-Dioulasso (Burkina Faso), Golf 3 (Togo), Marrakech (Morocco), Meknes (Morocco), Tetouan (Morocco), Thies (Senegal)
< 300 000	28	Al Hoceima (Morocco), Bama (Burkina Faso), Bangangte (Cameroon), Chefchaouen (Morocco), Dionaba (Mauritania), Kanembakache (Nigeria), Mbour (Senegal), Rosso (Mauritania), Saint-Louis (Senegal), Vogan (Togo)

Source: OECD (2021[1]), *OECD Survey on Water Governance in African Cities*, OECD, Paris.

The survey questionnaire (see Annex B) comprises 39 questions, distributed into 8 sections:

- Section 1: Megatrends and water risks.
- Section 2: Institutions in charge of water resource and water services management.
- Section 3: Coherence across local policies.
- Section 4: Financing.
- Section 5: Stakeholder engagement.
- Section 6: Data, monitoring, reporting, evaluation.
- Section 7: Obstacles to an effective water governance.
- Section 8: Future priorities for water policy.

The survey was sent out to local governments and city officials. The data from the survey were processed to assess water governance characteristics in African cities, provide quantified evidence regarding governance gaps and show the diversity of governance situations across African cities. Based on these responses, a series of city snapshots have been prepared to provide the granular data and facts for each respondent (see Chapter 4).

Dedicated water policies at the national and local levels in Africa

National Water Policy status in Africa

The United Nations (UN) Global Analysis and Assessment of Sanitation and Drinking-Water (GLAAS) report from 2019 provides information with regard to the adoption of national water and sanitation policies in African countries. In 28 African countries (64%), national water policies have been formally approved while they are undergoing revisions in 8 countries (18%) and are under development in 8 countries (18%). The situation is somewhat comparable for sanitation as 25 African countries (57%) have formally approved a national sanitation policy. In 8 countries, this policy is undergoing revisions and in 10 countries, (22%) it is under development. (Figure 2.2). Furthermore, in two-thirds of African countries, the human rights to water and sanitation are recognised in the constitution.

Figure 2.2. Existence of national water and sanitation policies in Africa, 2018/19

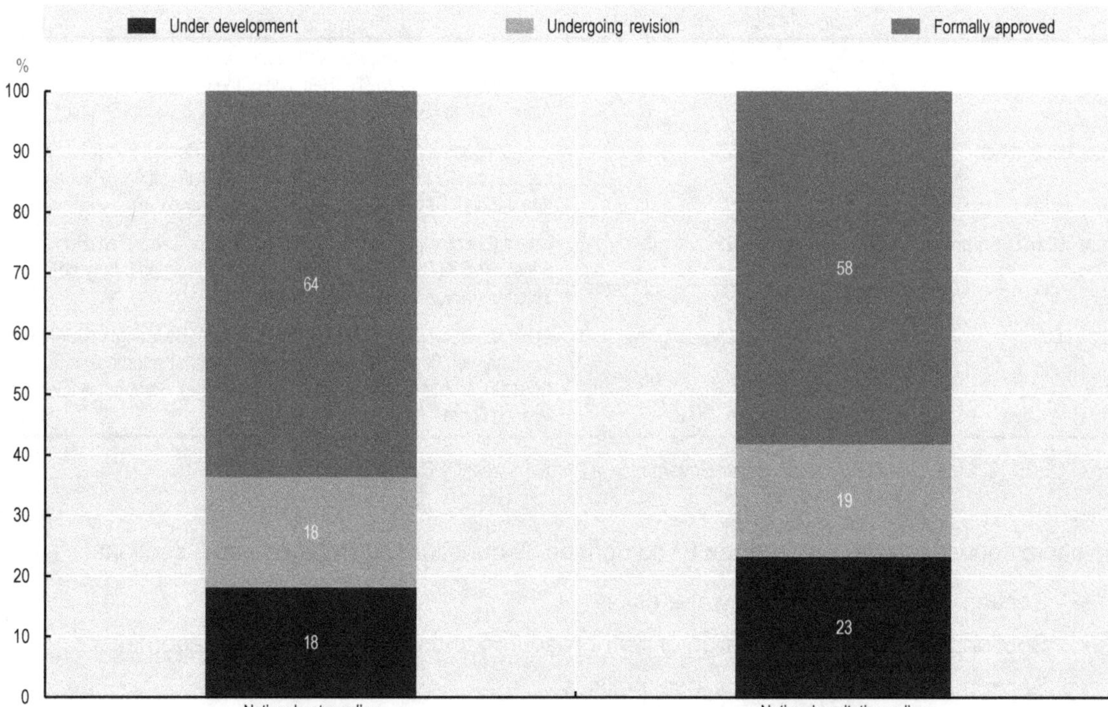

Note: Sample of 44 African countries for national water policy and 43 countries for national sanitation policy.
Source: UN-Water (2019[2]), *National Systems to Support Drinking-water, Sanitation and Hygiene – Global Status Report 2019*; UN-Water (2019[3]), *Global Analysis and Assessment of Sanitation and Drinking-Water (GLAAS) 2019 Report.*

The GLAAS reporting also shows that national plans are fully or partially implemented in 33 African countries (75%) for water and 27 countries (61%) for sanitation (Figure 2.3). Thirty-two African countries developed cost estimates of their water plans and 30 countries for their sanitation plans. However, a lot fewer countries have conducted human resources assessment for their water (18 countries) and sanitation (20 countries) plans. Furthermore, approximately half of the countries report that the financial and human resources they have are less than 50% of what is needed to effectively implement water and sanitation policies. Although two-thirds of African countries have developed agreed financial plans for water (68%) and sanitation (64%), these plans remain insufficiently used and implemented in most countries.

Local Water Policy status in Africa

In addition to national water and sanitation policies, African cities take greater leadership to address water-related issues at the local level by adopting and implementing dedicated water and sanitation policies. The OECD Survey on Water Governance in African Cities (2021[1]) shows that about three cities out of four in the respondents' sample have also adopted local dedicated water and sanitation policies, which include investment plans and programmes. In comparison, only half of the cities have adopted a local policy on water resources management.

Figure 2.3. Existence of national water and sanitation implementation plans in Africa, 2018/19

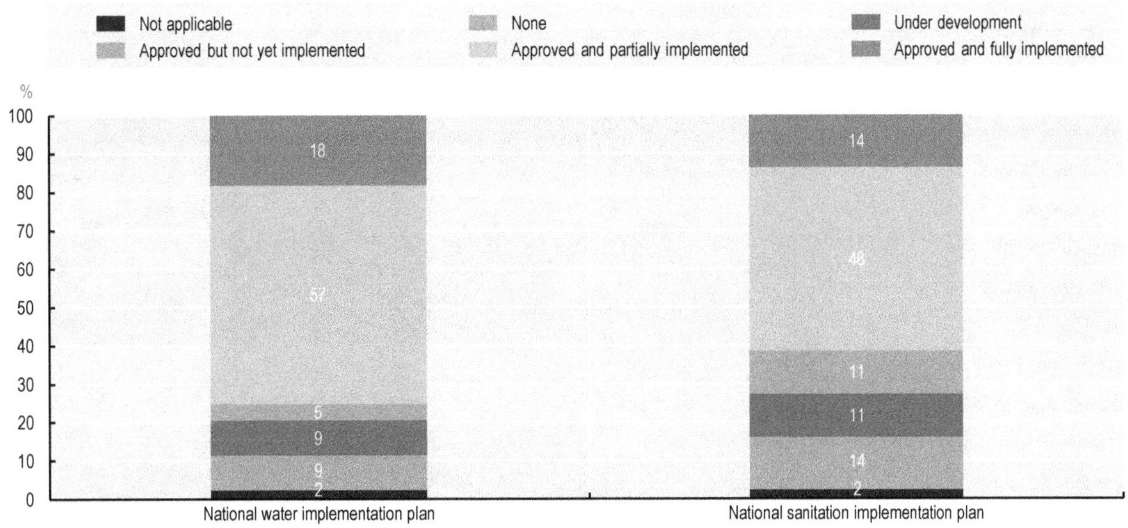

Note: Sample of 44 African countries.

Source: UN-Water (2019[2]), *National Systems to Support Drinking-water, Sanitation and Hygiene – Global Status Report 2019*; UN-Water (2019[3]), *Global Analysis and Assessment of Sanitation and Drinking-Water (GLAAS) 2019 Report*.

In general and where they exist, local water and sanitation policies tend to clearly indicate goals to reach and duties of the involved water institutions. On the contrary, they do not always clearly indicate the resources needed to achieve the goals, thus generating unfunded mandates hampering their implementation (Table 2.2 and Table 2.3). In addition, many local governments do not monitor nor evaluate policies implementation, lacking the setup of corrective actions whenever necessary, based on robust information. The findings are equivalent for local water resource policies.

Eighty percent of the cities that have adopted a local water resource policy have also developed a local dedicated water and sanitation policy. As such, these cities have developed a comprehensive local water policy thus avoiding a silo approach that often generates poor planning, a lack of policy coherence and misalignment of incentives. Within the sample of surveyed cities, six cities declare that they have adopted neither a local water and sanitation policy nor a local water resource policy, whereas another five cities did not provide an answer.

Table 2.2. African cities with a dedicated water and sanitation policy at the local level

Cities	Dedicated water and sanitation policy at the city level	Clear goals	Clear duties	Resources needed	Emergency strategies	Regularly monitored
Chefchaouen (Morocco)						
Al Hoceima (Morocco)						
Bangangte (Cameroon)						
Tetouan (Morocco)						
Tanger (Morocco)						
Fes (Morocco)						
Rabat (Morocco)						
Lusaka (Zambia)						
Cape Town (South Africa)						

Cities	Dedicated water and sanitation policy at the city level	Clear goals	Clear duties	Resources needed	Emergency strategies	Regularly monitored
Kampala (Uganda)	Yes	Yes	Yes	Yes	Yes	Yes
Accra (Ghana)	Yes	Yes	Yes	Yes	Yes	Yes
Kanembakache (Niger)	Yes	Yes	Yes	Yes	No	Yes
Saint-Louis (Senegal)	Yes	Yes	Yes	Yes	No	No
Thies (Senegal)	Yes	Yes	Yes	Yes	No	Yes
Meknes (Morocco)	Yes	Yes	Yes	No	Yes	No
Dionaba (Mauritania)	Yes	Yes	No	No	No	No
Vogan (Togo)	Yes	Yes	No	No	No	No
Bama (Burkina Faso)	Yes	Yes	No answer	No answer	No answer	No answer
Antananarivo (Madagascar)	Yes	Yes	No answer	No answer	No answer	No answer
Brazzaville (Republic of the Congo)	Yes	No	No	No	No	No
Nouakchott (Mauritania)	Yes	No	No	No	No	No
Lome (Togo)	Yes	No answer	No answer	No answer	No answer	No answer
Dakar (Senegal)	Yes	No answer	No answer	No answer	No answer	No answer
Marrakech (Morocco)	Yes	No answer	No answer	No answer	No answer	No answer
Mbour (Senegal)	No	No	No	No	No	No
Bobo-Dioulasso (Burkina Faso)	No	No	No	No	No	No
Cocody (Cote d'Ivoire)	No	No	No	No	No	No
Golf 3 (Togo)	No	No	No	No	No	No
Monrovia (Liberia)	No	No	No	No	No	No
Abidjan (Cote d'Ivoire)	No	No	No	No	No	No
Rosso (Mauritania)	No answer	No answer	No answer	No answer	No answer	No answer
Banjul (Gambia)	No answer	No answer	No answer	No answer	No answer	No answer
Bangui (Central African Republic)	No answer	No answer	No answer	No answer	No answer	No answer
Maputo (Mozambique)	No answer	No answer	No answer	No answer	No answer	No answer
Cotonou (Benin)	No answer	No answer	No answer	No answer	No answer	No answer
Abuja (Nigeria)	No answer	No answer	No answer	No answer	No answer	No answer

Note: 36 respondent cities to the question "has your city developed a dedicated water and sanitation policy at the local level".
Yes
No
No answer
Source: OECD (2021[1]), *OECD Survey on Water Governance in African Cities*, OECD, Paris.

Table 2.3. African cities with a dedicated water resources policy at the local level

Cities	Dedicated water resources policy at the city level	Clear goals	Clear duties	Resources needed	Climate resilience aspects	Regularly monitored
Bobo-Dioulasso (Burkina Faso)	Yes	Yes	Yes	Yes	Yes	Yes
Tetouan (Morocco)	Yes	Yes	Yes	Yes	Yes	Yes
Marrakech (Morocco)	Yes	Yes	Yes	Yes	Yes	Yes
Rabat (Morocco)	Yes	Yes	Yes	Yes	Yes	Yes
Saint-Louis (Senegal)	Yes	Yes	Yes	Yes	Yes	No

Cities	Dedicated water resources policy at the city level	Clear goals	Clear duties	Resources needed	Climate resilience aspects	Regularly monitored
Fes (Morocco)	Yes	Yes	Yes	Yes	Yes	No
Tanger (Morocco)	Yes	Yes	Yes	Yes	No	Yes
Lusaka (Zambia)	Yes	Yes	Yes	Yes	No	Yes
Meknes (Morocco)	Yes	Yes	Yes	No	Yes	No
Cotonou (Benin)	Yes	Yes	Yes	No	Yes	No
Bangangte (Cameroon)	Yes	Yes	Yes	No	No	No
Cape Town (South Africa)	Yes	Yes	No	No	Yes	Yes
Bama (Burkina Faso)	Yes	No answer	No answer	No answer	Yes	No answer
Nouakchott (Mauritania)	Yes	No answer	No answer	No answer	No answer	No answer
Lome (Togo)	Yes	No answer	No answer	No answer	No answer	No answer
Dionaba (Mauritania)	No	No	No	No	No	No
Vogan (Togo)	No	No	No	No	No	No
Kanembakache (Niger)	No	No	No	No	No	No
Al Hoceima (Morocco)	No	No	No	No	No	No
Mbour (Senegal)	No	No	No	No	No	No
Cocody (Cote d'Ivoire)	No	No	No	No	No	No
Golf 3 (Togo)	No	No	No	No	No	No
Thies (Senegal)	No	No	No	No	No	No
Monrovia (Liberia)	No	No	No	No	No	No
Dakar (Senegal)	No	No	No	No	No	No
Kampala (Uganda)	No	No	No	No	No	No
Abidjan (Cote d'Ivoire)	No	No	No	No	No	No
Accra (Ghana)	No	No	No	No	No	No
Brazzaville (Republic of the Congo)	No	No	No	No	No	No
Chefchaouen (Morocco)	No answer	No answer	No answer	No answer	No answer	No answer
Rosso (Mauritania)	No answer	No answer	No answer	No answer	No answer	No answer
Banjul (Gambia)	No answer	No answer	No answer	No answer	No answer	No answer
Bangui (Central African Republic)	No answer	No answer	No answer	No answer	No answer	No answer
Maputo (Mozambique)	No answer	No answer	No answer	No answer	No answer	No answer
Abuja (Nigeria)	No answer	No answer	No answer	No answer	No answer	No answer
Antananarivo (Madagascar)	No answer	No answer	No answer	No answer	No answer	No answer

Note: 36 cities responded to the question "Has your city developed an explicit water resources policy at the local level?".

Yes

No

No answer

Source: OECD (2021[1]), *OECD Survey on Water Governance in African Cities*, OECD, Paris.

Social and pro-poor measures in water policies in Africa

Examples of dedicated water and sanitation policies at the local level include for instance generic social measures and targeted provisions towards vulnerable categories of population. Indeed, half of the respondent cities have set up measures to guarantee a minimum water volume for basic needs, whether these measures derive from national or local policies. As an illustration, this volume amounts to 7 m³/capita in Benin, 55 l/capita/day in Brazzaville (Republic of the Congo) and 10.5 m³/household/month in Cape Town (South Africa). Furthermore 79% of the surveyed cities are implementing social measures with regard to access to water and sanitation services (Figure 2.4). These measures take the form of a social water or/and sanitation tariff (27%) or a social connection rate (14%), or both (55%). In Senegal, the national water provider SONES has set up a social connection programme allowing low-income customers to have access to the network for free whereas the average cost exceeds XOF 100 000. To date, more than 200 000 social connections have been installed, as well as 1 500 standpipes.

Figure 2.4. Social tariffs for vulnerable categories in surveyed African cities

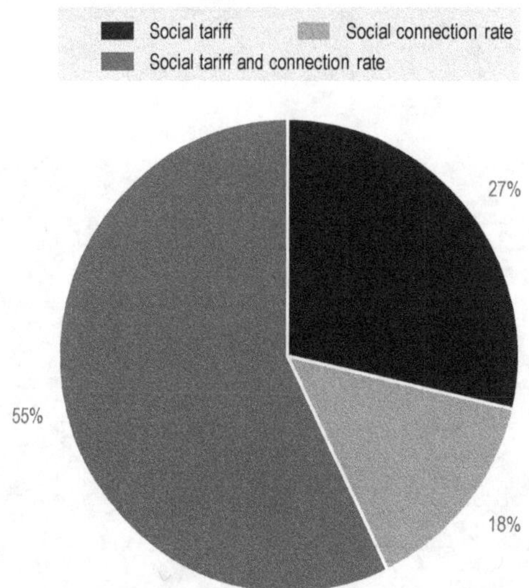

Note: 28 cities responded to the question "At the city level, are there social measures for vulnerable categories of water and/or sanitation users?".
Source: OECD (2021[1]), *OECD Survey on Water Governance in African Cities*, OECD, Paris.

The GLAAS report states that almost all African countries have adopted water and sanitation national policies and measures to reach poor populations. The situation is more nuanced with regard to affordability schemes. Thirty-four African countries (in a sample of 44) have set such schemes for water supply but only half of them are reported to be widely used, while another 7 countries have not established any affordability scheme.

In addition to social tariffs or connection fees, cities have implemented other explicit measures at the local level to guarantee access to water and/or sanitation services to vulnerable groups. In 58% of the surveyed cities, these measures are targeted towards the poor population and, in 42% of the cases, they are targeted towards population living in informal settlements which can represent up to three-quarters of the city's overall population. In one-third of the cities, some measures concern indigenous peoples and ethnic minorities, or people living with disabilities. Women or female-headed households benefit from specific measures in 14% of the surveyed cities only. The latter raises particular challenges in terms of gender and inclusion overall since in many countries, women and girls are tasked with the management of household water supply, sanitation and health as they are often in charge of food production and preparation, care of domestic animals, personal hygiene, care of the sick, cleaning, washing and waste disposal (Box 2.2).

Access to safe and sufficient water supply and improved sanitation facilities has a heavy impact on the lives of women and girls. In the absence of such access, they have to discharge related difficult and time-consuming tasks, which precludes other occupations or participation in education. It also puts women at risk of abuse and attacks while walking to and using a toilet or open defecation site, as they have specific hygiene needs during menstruation, pregnancy and child rearing.

Box 2.2. Water access and gender inequality

In urban areas of Africa, more than half the urban population is forced to use a collective water source, usually a standpipe, a pump or, less frequently, a well (WHO/UNICEF, 2015[4]). This requires a large amount of time to travel to the water collection point, wait at the water source, transport the water and store it. Aligned with socially-constructed gender roles, the burden of water collection and storage usually falls on women and girls. In sub-Saharan Africa, it is estimated that women and girls spend about 40 billion hours per year transporting water (UNDP, 2006[5]). For example, a study conducted in the informal settlements of Ouagadougou in Burkina Faso shows that females are responsible for water collection in 84% of households sampled (Dos Santos S, 2016[6]). This study showed that male household water collectors often use standpipes while female collectors preferred boreholes, despite the latter requiring significant physical effort. Women's preference for this type of supply is explained both by economic factors (water at boreholes is cheaper than water at standpipes) and by distance: women, who are less likely to have motorised transport than men, prefer boreholes that are often less remote from the dwellings than the standpipes located in the formal zones. More studies are needed to systematically document household gender-water relations in informal settlements and how this may reinforce inequalities in water access.

Source: Santos, S. et al. (2017[7]), "Urban growth and water access in sub-Saharan Africa: Progress, challenges and emerging research directions", *Science of the Total Environment*, Vol. 607-608, Elsevier, pp. 497-508.

At the local level, gender-sensitive approaches that involve women at design, implementation and management phases are proving successful to improve the suitability, sustainability and reach of water and sanitation services. Embedding further gender equity into policies at all levels will be crucial to achieving many parts of the UN Sustainable Development Goal (SDG) agenda. One illustrative case is that of the Obudu Plateau in Nigeria, where the construction of a tourist resort exacerbated existing pressures and tensions around water resources (Majekodunmi, 2006[8]). As a result, the Nigerian Conservation Foundation implemented a Watershed Management Project in 1999. Women were included throughout all stages, including the design, implementation and monitoring of the project, and elected to the management committee. This allowed the resolution of a water conflict between the Becheve women and the Fulani herdsmen, and reduced diarrhoea cases by 45%. The considerable reduction in the time needed to collect water also gave women more time for income-generating activities such as farming as well as other activities, in addition to increasing the rate of school attendance for girls. The World Bank Rural Water Supply and Sanitation Project, carried out in 6 Moroccan provinces, reduced the time spent by women and girls collecting water by between 50% and 90% (World Bank, 2003[9]). As a result, the school attendance of girls in these provinces increased by 20% in 4 years.

Institutions in charge of water at the national and local levels in Africa

Water and sanitation provision responsibility commonly centralised at the national level in Africa

In a majority of African countries, water policy is driven at the national level by a line ministry. A large number of African countries have also set up national water service providers, thus amplifying further the leadership of the national level over water policies (Figure 2.5). As an illustration, in 71% of the countries where respondent cities from the OECD survey sample are located, the national level is responsible for the provision of water supply and sanitation (WSS) services throughout the country's territory (Table 2.2).

Another consequence of this centralised institutional setting is that the national level is also in charge of most regulatory functions including tariff setting, quality standards definition and monitoring, and consumer protection and engagement. As a result, 78% of the surveyed cities reported not having any control over their water tariffs and two-thirds not overseeing any water utility business plan.

Figure 2.5. Levels of government responsible for water service provision in select African countries

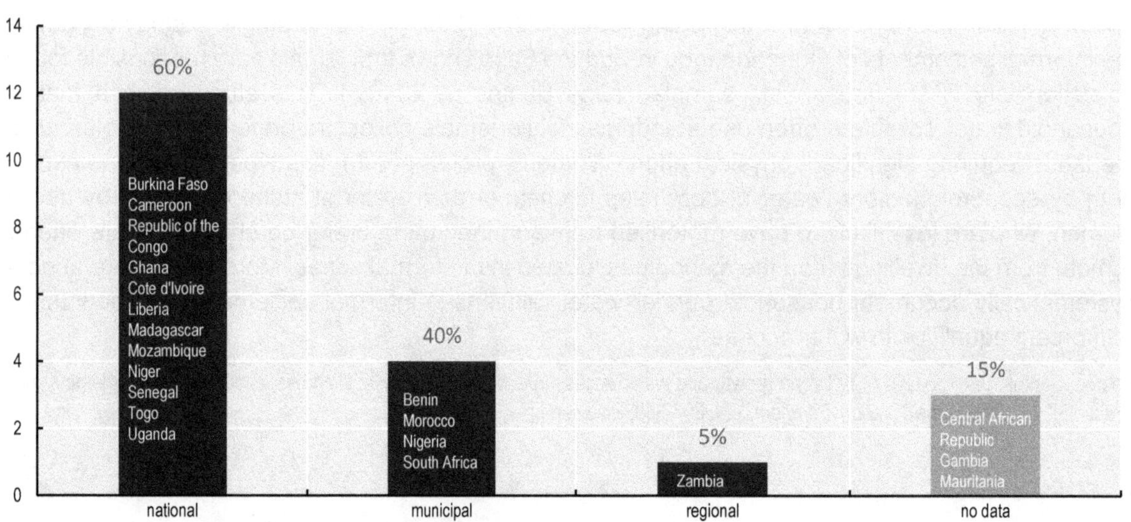

Note: Sample of 20 countries comprising all 36 surveyed cities.
Source: Author's elaboration based on World Bank (n.d.[10]), *World Bank Aggregation Toolkit (interactive map)*, https://www.worldbank.org/en/topic/water/publication/water-aggregation-toolkit.

Characteristics of water and sanitation utilities in Africa

The OECD survey results provide further information regarding some characteristics of WSS utilities in African cities:

- There is a predominance of single operators for service provision at the city level, whether it be a municipal or a national service provider.

Table 2.4. Number of water and sanitation service providers per surveyed cities

Cities	Number of water service providers	Number of sanitation service providers
Meknes (Morocco)		
Al Hoceima (Morocco)		
Abidjan (Côte d'Ivoire)		
Tanger (Morocco)		
Rabat (Morocco)		
Cape Town (South Africa)		
Lusaka (Zambia)		
Antananarivo (Madagascar)		
Bangui (Central African Republic)		
Tetouan (Morocco)		

Cities	Number of water service providers	Number of sanitation service providers
Cocody (Côte d'Ivoire)	A single service provider	A single service provider
Saint-Louis (Senegal)	A single service provider	A single service provider
Thies (Senegal)	A single service provider	A single service provider
Mbour (Senegal)	A single service provider	A single service provider
Dakar (Senegal)	A single service provider	A single service provider
Nouakchott (Mauritania)	A single service provider	A single service provider
Chefchaouen (Morocco)	A single service provider	A single service provider
Bobo-Dioulasso (Burkina Faso)	A single service provider	A single service provider
Bama (Burkina Faso)	A single service provider	A single service provider
Banjul (Gambia)	A single service provider	A single service provider
Vogan (Togo)	A single service provider	No answer
Kanembakache (Niger)	A single service provider	No answer
Cotonou (Benin)	A single service provider	No answer
Dionaba (Mauritania)	A single service provider	No answer
Fes (Morocco)	Several service providers	A single service provider
Marrakech (Morocco)	Several service providers	A single service provider
Rosso (Mauritania)	Several service providers	A single service provider
Accra (Ghana)	Several service providers	Several service providers
Maputo (Mozambique)	Several service providers	Several service providers
Bangangte (Cameroon)	Several service providers	Several service providers
Lome (Togo)	Several service providers	Several service providers
Golf 3 (Togo)	Several service providers	Several service providers
Brazzaville (Republic of the Congo)	Several service providers	Several service providers
Kampala (Uganda)	No answer	Several service providers
Monrovia (Liberia)	No answer	No answer
Abuja (Nigeria)	No answer	No answer

Note: 36 cities responded to the question "How many formal service providers operate in your city's administrative boundaries?".
A single service provider
Several service providers
No answer
Source: OECD (2021[1]), *OECD Survey on Water Governance in African Cities*, OECD, Paris.

- Utilities are operated by public operators in two-thirds of the surveyed cities. Private operators are running services in about a quarter of the respondent cities, while in the remaining ones, services are operated by a mix of public and private operators.

A great diversity of water and sanitation access forms in African cities

- Nine cities out of ten declare to be delivering water mainly through in-house domestic connections and public standpipes. Access to water through shared yard-tap connections is also widespread in two-thirds of the cities, as well as boreholes and wells. In the case of water shortage, some formal water providers resort to delivering water through tanker trucks or bottled water (Figure 2.6).

Figure 2.6. Water access forms in surveyed cities

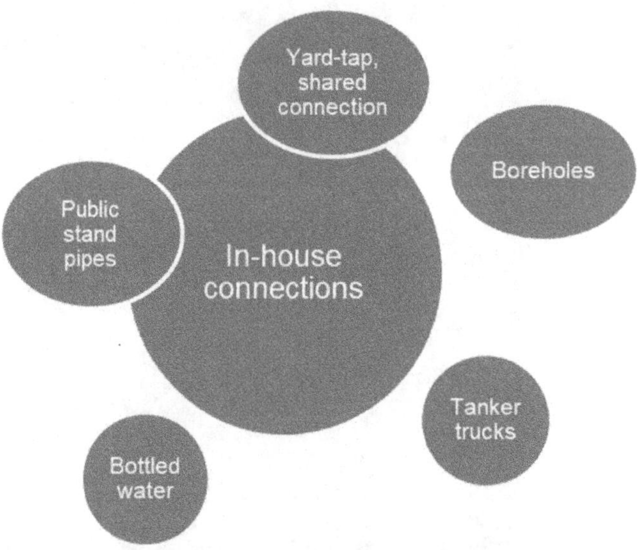

Source: OECD (2021[1]), *OECD Survey on Water Governance in African Cities*, OECD, Paris.

This variety of water access forms illustrates the capacity of local governments to develop tailor-made and place-based responses. This includes the ability to adapt service quality standards to local needs and the specific context of disfavoured neighbourhoods and vulnerable urban areas. Initiatives such as flow limiters, the use of plastic-bodied water meters, ground tanks and semi-pressure water service levels, were first introduced to South Africa by the water service of eThekwini (Box 2.3) in order to provide water supply in informal settlements. At the same time, this diversity of access forms generates some co-ordination and regulation challenges. For instance, in Cape Town during the water crisis, many residents and businesses developed alternative water supplies including drilling private boreholes, in response to the severe water restrictions and penalty tariffs for high volume consumers decided by the city. The legal status of these boreholes was poorly defined (guidelines were issued in 2018 by the National Department for Water and Sanitation) and they have led to over-abstraction, illegal resale of water, inadequate water quality compliance and difficulties to get people to register their boreholes through the online registry. Unregulated boreholes are likely to pose a long-term threat to the recharge and sustainability of underground water bodies, as well as quality issues due to possible contaminated aquifers in the absence of protected areas. Moreover, the unregulated use of groundwater is competing with legal use granted through water licences.

Box 2.3. Adapting quality standards in eThekwini, South Africa

In eThekwini, South Africa, Durban Metro Water Services experimented with alternative service standards in order to meet the needs of customers in poor areas. Varying quality standards were proposed to customers so that they could choose between a range of options with differentiated price/quality characteristics. For example, eThekwini Metro Water Services developed semi-pressurised water systems with the provision of a roof tank as an alternative to a full pressurised system (which may be unaffordable). In such a system, water is reticulated using small diameter piping, which is laid along the major access routes or tracks located within the informal area. At appropriate intervals, connections are made to this reticulation and a manifold, which allows approximately 20 houses to connect to the water main, is installed. Each consumer receives a 200-litre water tank that is serviced by a water bailiff every day. This system results in a low level of unaccounted-for water because of the low pressure and effective customer demand management. Overall water consumption through such a service delivery system is estimated to be up to 50% less than conventional systems to communities of similar profile. The approach nevertheless provides sufficient water to households to maintain a basic level of hygiene and health. In areas where this system could not be installed, standpipes/water dispensers are provided to supply informal communities as an interim measure. Furthermore, water sachets or tankered water are supplied in the case of prolonged service interruptions. Finally, water boreholes are available where there is no water reticulation.

Source: World Bank (2006[11]), "Taking account of the poor in water sector regulation", *Water Supply & Sanitation Working Notes*, No. 11, World Bank, Washington, DC; eThekwini Municipality (2019[12]), *eThekwini Water and Sanitation Service Level Standards, 13th edition, July 2019/2020*.

- In three cities out of four, formal sanitation service is provided through flush or pour-flush to piped sewers,[1] or to open drain mainly in disadvantaged neighbourhoods. More than half of the cities also provide access to sanitation through a ventilated improved pit, and one-third through open pits (Figure 2.7).

Figure 2.7. Sanitation service delivery forms in surveyed cities

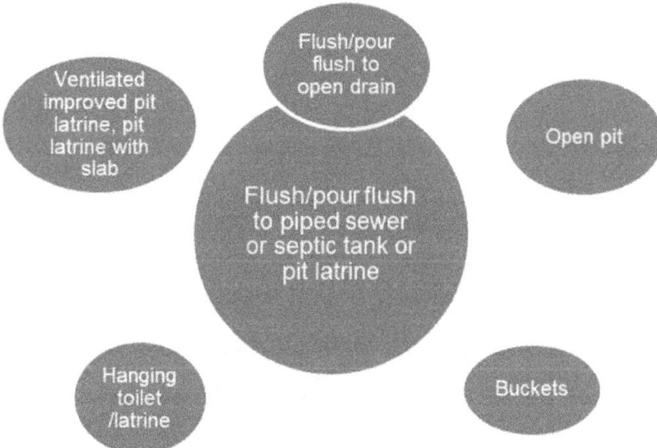

Source: OECD (2021[1]), *OECD Survey on Water Governance in African Cities*, OECD, Paris.

References

Dos Santos S, W. (2016), *Les Objectifs du Millénaire pour le Développement, l'accès à l'eau et les rapports de genre*, pp. 63-78. [6]

eThekwini Municipality (2019), *eThekwini Water and Sanitation Service Level Standards, 13th edition, July 2019/2020.* [12]

Majekodunmi, A. (2006), *Using Gender Mainstreaming Processes to Help Protect Drinking.* [8]

OECD (2021), *OECD Survey on Water Governance in African Cities*, OECD, Paris. [1]

Santos, S. et al. (2017), "Urban growth and water access in sub-Saharan Africa: Progress, challenges, and emerging research directions", *Science of the Total Environment*, Vol. 607-608, pp. 497-508. [7]

UNDP (2006), *Human Development Report 2006. Beyond scarcity: Power, poverty and the global water crisis.* [5]

UN-Water (2019), *Global Analysis and Assessment of Sanitation and Drinking-Water (GLAAS) 2019 Report*, United Nations. [3]

UN-Water (2019), *National Systems to Support Drinking-water, Sanitation and Hygiene – Global Status Report 2019*, United Nations. [2]

WHO/UNICEF (2015), *Progress on sanitation and drinking water: 2015 update and MDG assessment*, http://apps.who.int/iris/bitstream/10665/177752/1/9789241509145_eng.pdf. [4]

World Bank (2006), "Taking account of the poor in water sector regulation", *Water Supply & Sanitation Working Notes*, No. 11, World Bank, Washington, DC. [11]

World Bank (2003), *Implementation Completion Report. Report No. 25917.* [9]

World Bank (n.d.), *World Bank Aggregation Toolkit (interactive map)*, https://www.worldbank.org/en/topic/water/publication/water-aggregation-toolkit. [10]

Note

[1] The survey included the following sanitation categories: flush/pour-flush to piped sewer, or to septic tank, or to pit latrine or to open drain; ventilated improved pit latrine, pit latrine with slab; open pit; buckets; hanging toilet/latrine.

3 Water governance challenges in African cities

This chapter analyses the key governance challenges for water resources management and water and sanitation services in African countries and cities. The chapter uses the OECD Principles on Water Governance to assess key issues related to scale mismatch, policy coherence, data, monitoring and evaluation, funding, transparency and integrity, and stakeholder engagement.

The OECD Principles on Water Governance aim to enhance water governance systems that help manage "too much", "too little" and "too polluted" water and foster universal access to drinking water and sanitation, in a sustainable, integrated and inclusive way, at an acceptable cost and in a reasonable time frame. The principles acknowledge that good governance is a means to an end to master complexity and managing trade-offs in a policy domain that is highly sensitive to fragmentation, silos, scale mismatch, negative externalities, monopolies and large capital-intensive investment. They consider that governance is good if it can help to solve key water challenges, using a combination of bottom-up and top-down processes while fostering constructive state-society relations. It is bad if it generates undue transaction costs and does not respond to place-based needs. The OECD Principles on Water Governance intend to contribute to tangible and outcome-oriented public policies, based on three mutually reinforcing and complementary dimensions of water governance (Box 3.1).

This chapter uses the 12 OECD Principles on Water Governance to assess a number of key governance challenges for water resources management and water and sanitation services in African cities. The following sections put particular emphasis on issues related to scale mismatch, policy coherence, data and evaluation, funding, integrity and transparency and stakeholder engagement. Issues related to Principle 1 on institutional fragmentation were covered under Chapter 2. Principle 8 on innovative water governance practices could not be appraised because of lack of data from city respondents. Principle 7 on regulatory frameworks is not investigated either because of the highly centralised regulatory frameworks in African countries and the rather limited prerogatives at the local level. Finally, Principle 4 on capacity is covered in a cross-cutting fashion under the specific governance gaps hereinafter analysed.

Box 3.1. The OECD Principles on Water Governance

The OECD Principles on Water Governance intend to contribute to tangible and outcome-oriented public policies, based on three mutually reinforcing and complementary dimensions of water governance (Figure 3.1).

1. Effectiveness relates to the contribution of governance to define clear sustainable water policy goals and targets at all levels of government, to implement those policy goals and to meet expected targets.
2. Efficiency relates to the contribution of governance to maximise the benefits of sustainable water management and welfare at the least cost to society.
3. Trust and engagement relate to the contribution of governance to building public confidence and ensuring the inclusiveness of stakeholders through democratic legitimacy and fairness for society at large.

Enhancing the effectiveness of water governance

- Principle 1. Clearly allocate and distinguish roles and responsibilities for water policymaking, policy implementation, operational management and regulation, and foster co-ordination across these responsible authorities.
- Principle 2. Manage water at the appropriate scale(s) within integrated basin governance systems to reflect local conditions and foster co-ordination between the different scales.
- Principle 3. Encourage policy coherence through effective cross-sectoral co-ordination, especially between policies for water and the environment, health, energy, agriculture, industry, spatial planning and land use.
- Principle 4. Adapt the level of capacity of responsible authorities to the complexity of water challenges to be met and to the set of competencies required to carry out their duties.

Figure 3.1. Overview of OECD Principles on Water Governance

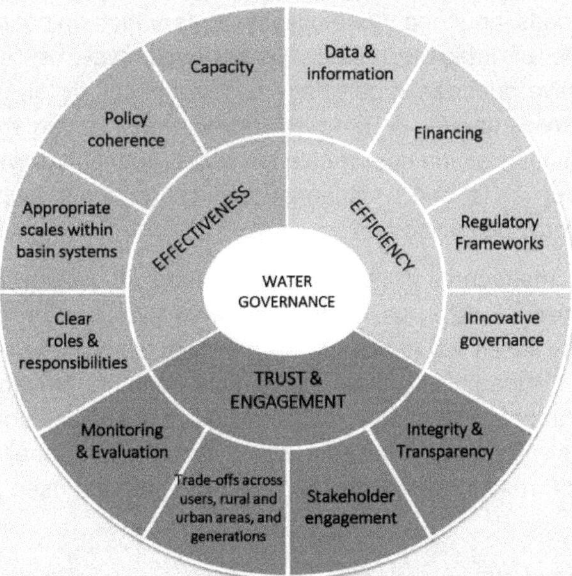

Source: OECD (2015[1]), *OECD Principles on Water Governance*, https://www.oecd.org/gov/regional-policy/OECD-Principles-on-Water-Governancebrochure.pdf.

Enhancing the efficiency of water governance

- Principle 5. Produce, update and share timely, consistent, comparable and policy-relevant water and water-related data and information, and use it to guide, assess and improve water policy.
- Principle 6. Ensure that governance arrangements help mobilise water finance and allocate financial resources in an efficient, transparent and timely manner.
- Principle 7. Ensure that sound water management regulatory frameworks are effectively implemented and enforced in pursuit of the public interest.
- Principle 8. Promote the adoption and implementation of innovative water governance practices across responsible authorities, levels of government and relevant stakeholders.

Enhancing trust and engagement in water governance

- Principle 9. Mainstream integrity and transparency practices across water policies, water institutions and water governance frameworks for greater accountability and trust in decision-making.
- Principle 10. Promote stakeholder engagement for informed and outcome-oriented contributions to water policy design and implementation.
- Principle 11. Encourage water governance frameworks that help manage trade-offs across water users, rural and urban areas, and generations.
- Principle 12. Promote regular monitoring and evaluation of water policy and governance where appropriate, share the results with the public and make adjustments when needed.

Source: OECD (2015[1]), *OECD Principles on Water Governance*, https://www.oecd.org/gov/regional-policy/OECD-Principles-on-Water-Governancebrochure.pdf.

Managing water at the appropriate scale

Weak articulation between institutional, functional and hydrological logics affects urban water management because cities sit on watersheds, bounded hydrologic systems, which do not correspond to administrative perimeters. In the absence of integrated basin governance systems, such a mismatch between hydrological and administrative boundaries can have consequences in terms of competition over water uses and effectiveness of service delivery. In order to address water governance properly, there is a need to consider the territorial continuity as the basin scale links upstream and downstream communities. In the case of water, beyond the functional and institutional/administrative perspectives, the watershed, which follows hydrological logics, must be considered.

Integrated water resource management (IWRM) is "a process, which promotes the co-ordinated development and management of water, land and related resources, in order to maximise the resultant economic and social welfare in an equitable manner without compromising the sustainability of vital ecosystems" (Global Water Partnership, 2000[2]). By bringing together stakeholders from various sectors and across levels of government, IWRM promotes the co-ordinated development and management of water, thus providing a holistic framework for addressing water-related challenges. At their core, IWRM frameworks ensure that water resources are developed, managed and used in an equitable, sustainable and efficient manner.

OECD Water Governance Principle n°2 on Appropriate Scale(s)

Manage water at the appropriate scale(s) within integrated basin governance systems to reflect local conditions and foster co-ordination between the different scales. To that effect, water management practices and tools should:

1. Respond to long-term environmental, economic and social objectives with a view to making the best use of water resources, through risk prevention and IWRM.
2. Encourage sound hydrological cycle management from capture and distribution of freshwater to the release of wastewater and return flows.
3. Promote adaptive and mitigation strategies, action programmes and measures based on clear and coherent mandates, through effective basin management plans that are consistent with national policies and local conditions.
4. Promote multi-level co-operation among users, stakeholders and levels of government for the management of water resources.
5. Enhance riparian co-operation on the use of transboundary freshwater resources.

Source: OECD (2015[1]), *OECD Principles on Water Governance*, https://www.oecd.org/gov/regional-policy/OECD-Principles-on-Water-Governancebrochure.pdf.

The reporting of United Nations (UN) Sustainable Development Goal (SDG) 6.5.1 on "implementation of integrated water resources management" shows that 42 African countries (82%) have adopted IWRM based policies, laws and plans at the national level, thus establishing an enabling environment to support IWRM implementation. However, at the subnational level, only 45% of African countries have approved plans for most of their basins or aquifers. Furthermore, progress is lowest at the basin/aquifer level when comparing the seven enabling environment IWRM elements (Figure 3.2).

Figure 3.2. IWRM monitoring in Africa (dimension 1 of SDG 6.5.1), 2017

Percentage of countries per implementation category

	Ave. Score
National policies (1.1a)	51
National laws (1.1b)	51
National plans (1.1c)	43
Basin/aquifer plans (1.2b)	34
Transboundary arrangements (1.2c)	58
Subnational policies (1.2a)	40
Provincial laws (federal countries) (1.2d)	27
Dimension 1. Enabling environment (average)	46

0% 20% 40% 60% 80% 100%

Implementation: Very low Low Medium-low Medium-high High Very high

Source: AMCOW (2018[3]), *Status Report on the Implementation of Integrated Water Resources Management in Africa: A Regional Report for SDG Indicator 6.5.1 on IWRM Implementation.*

While some IWRM institutional arrangements are in place in most African countries, implementation of such arrangements remains limited, with generally low capacity, geographic coverage and stakeholder participation. More than half of African countries (53%) have "medium-low" implementation of IRWM (AMCOW, 2018[3]). Important variations are noted between countries and regions across Africa, Northern and Southern Africa having higher levels of IWRM implementation than other African regions.

The SDG 6.5.1 monitoring shows that approximately 55% of African countries either have no basin or aquifer plans or are currently developing them (Figure 3.3). Furthermore, too few African cities and basins count with water allocation regimes, which, along with the limited participation of local governments into river basin committees, can threaten sustainable urban water resource management.

Figure 3.3. Basin management plans status in Africa

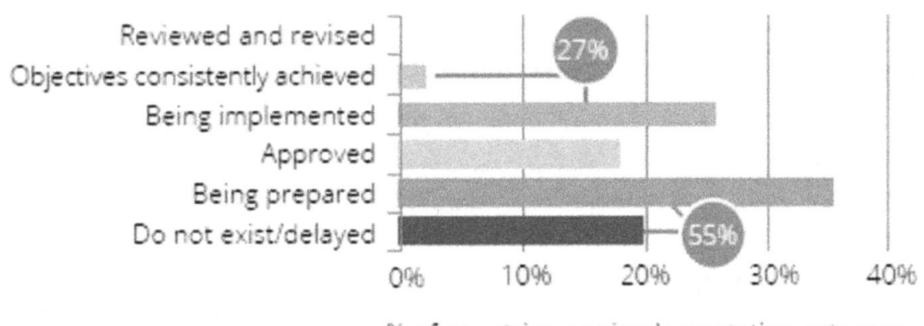

Source: AMCOW (2018[3]), *Status Report on the Implementation of Integrated Water Resources Management in Africa: A Regional Report for SDG Indicator 6.5.1 on IWRM Implementation.*

Finally, the SDG 6 reporting for Africa concludes that 71% of countries are unlikely to meet the global target of SDG 6.5.1 by 2030 unless progress is significantly accelerated. To improve IWRM implementation, African countries should increase efforts to establish and support groundwater and river basin institutions following the successful examples of the International Commission of the Congo-Oubangui-Sangha Basin or the Organisation for the Development of the Senegal River (Box 3.2).

Box 3.2. Examples of river basin organisations in Africa

The International Commission for the Congo-Oubangui-Sangha Basin (CICOS)

The agreement establishing a uniform river regime and creating CICOS and its addendum, signed on 21 November 1999 and 22 February 2007 respectively, entrust CICOS with two main missions:

- The promotion of inland navigation.
- Integrated management of water resources.

The jurisdiction of CICOS is the entire Congo River watershed located in the territories of member states (Angola, Cameroon, Central African Republic, Republic of the Congo, Democratic Republic of the Congo and Gabon).

In order to carry out these missions, CICOS has set itself the following objectives:

- Ensure the sustainable management of inland waterways.
- Harmonise the regulations on river transport for the safety of navigation and the promotion of the environment.
- Integrate all uses of water resources into regional planning.
- Optimise water allocations by use.
- Share among states the benefits generated by the uses of water.
- Support the development and fight against poverty in the sub-region.
- Promote food security.

Source: CICOS (n.d.[4]), *Homepage*, https://www.cicos.int/.

The Organisation for the Development of the Senegal River (OMVS)

The OMVS is an organisation gathering Guinea, Mali, Mauritania and Senegal for the purpose of jointly managing the Senegal River and its basin.

The Nouakchott Declaration adopted in 2003 by the 13th Conference of Heads of State and Government of the OMVS re-specified the missions of the organisation:

- The continuation and execution of ongoing programmes and projects by enhancing their integrative character.
- Methodological innovation through the search for sustainability while guaranteeing overall cohesion.
- The enhancement of human resources and the modernisation of management tools through increased use and genuine mastery of new information and communication technologies.
- The pursuit of sustainable development actions aimed at the triptych: economic growth, social progress and preservation of the environment.

The OMVS recently received a high score of 91 (for a maximum score of 100) in the Water Cooperation Quotient, which examines active co-operation by riparian countries in the management of water resources using ten parameters, including legal, political, technical, environmental, economic and institutional aspects.

Source: OMVS (n.d.[5]), *Homepage*, https://www.omvs.org/.

The state of play of IWRM at the national level in African countries is mirrored at the subnational level. The results of the OECD Survey on Water Governance in 36 African cities show that approximately two-thirds of the surveyed cities are not part of any river basin organisation and as such do not take part in water resource management decision-making at the river basin level. River basin organisations are important tools for co-ordinating water policy at the territorial level, across sectors, stakeholders and between levels of government. Indeed, they can be useful to: manage water at the appropriate scale through integrated basin governance to reflect local conditions and foster multi-level co-operation for the management of water resources; encourage sound hydrological cycle management; and promote adaptive and mitigation strategies.

Beyond river basin organisation, some surveyed cities declare that they use other co-ordination tools or institutions to co-ordinate urban water policy across levels of government and stakeholders. For instance, they take part in co-ordination platforms between local authorities and utilities (44%) or inter-municipal co-operation (36%).

Ensuring cross-sectoral policy coherence

As many decisions affecting urban water management are taken outside the water arena and vice-versa (spatial planning, agriculture, energy, etc.), co-ordination is essential to ensure a whole-of-government approach through which water can become a factor for sustainable growth and contribute to the broader economic, social and environmental agenda. On the contrary, conflicting objectives and rationalities compromise long-term targets for integrated urban water policy and cross-sectoral co-ordination. This can happen either because of diverging interests between water-related fields or because of scarce vertical and horizontal co-ordination across levels of government.

OECD Water Governance Principle n°3 on Policy Coherence

Encourage policy coherence through effective cross-sectoral co-ordination, especially between policies for water and the environment, health, energy, agriculture, industry, spatial planning and land use through:

1. Encouraging co-ordination mechanisms to facilitate coherent policies across ministries, public agencies and levels of government, including cross-sectoral plans.
2. Fostering co-ordinated management of use, protection and clean-up of water resources, taking into account policies that affect water availability, quality and demand (e.g. agriculture, forestry, mining, energy, fisheries, transportation, recreation and navigation) as well as risk prevention.
3. Identifying, assessing and addressing the barriers to policy coherence from practices, policies and regulations within and beyond the water sector, using monitoring, reporting and reviews.
4. Providing incentives and regulations to mitigate conflicts among sectoral strategies, bringing these strategies into line with water management needs and finding solutions that fit with local governance and norms.

Source: OECD (2015[1]), *OECD Principles on Water Governance*, https://www.oecd.org/gov/regional-policy/OECD-Principles-on-Water-Governancebrochure.pdf.

According to the OECD survey responses, land use and spatial planning are the sectoral policies that most affect urban water management, followed by public health, building codes and solid waste (Figure 3.4). A third of the surveyed cities have put in place a range of cross-sectoral co-ordination tools to foster policy coherence in these different domains comprising joint planning or programmes, partnerships, a platform for dialogue, co-ordination groups, or contracts.

Figure 3.4. Most influential policy areas on urban water management in surveyed cities

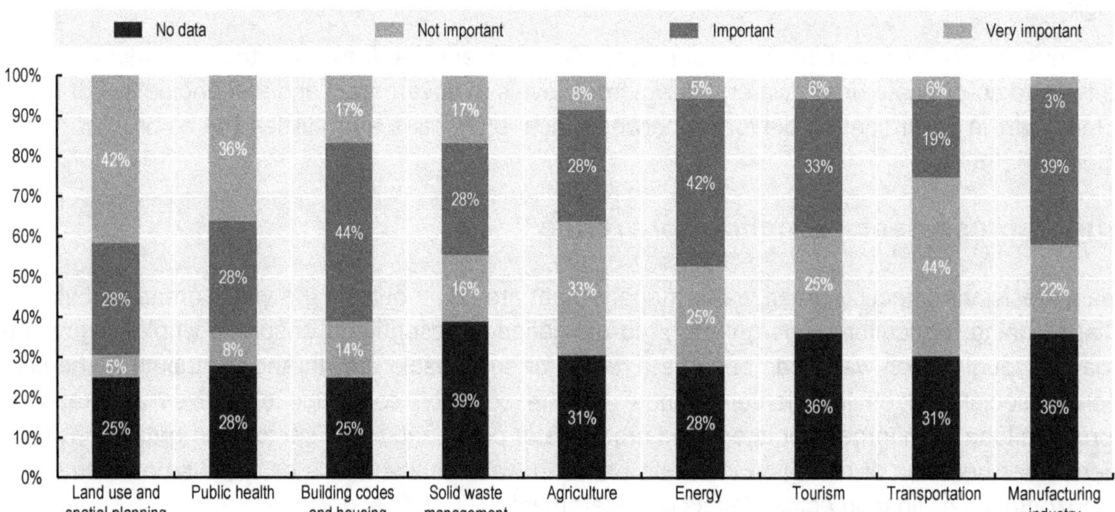

Note: 36 cities responded to the question "How important is the influence of the following policy areas on urban water management in your city?".

Source: OECD (2021[6]), *OECD Survey on Water Governance in African Cities*, OECD, Paris.

In the following sections, a specific zoom is provided on the influence of policies related to land use and spatial planning, public health and solid waste on water-related policies.

Land use

Land use policy and water policy are intertwined. The alteration of landscape affects water resources availability, quality and quantity. Ecosystems functions are heavily impaired when land use is modified. For example, where previously forested slopes retained soil sediment and moisture, conversion to agriculture may reduce dry season stream flows and generate higher sediment runoff, soil erosion or diffuse pollution. Sub-Saharan Africa is the region that has lost the largest share of its forest land (12%) over the past 25 years.

Conversion of land into built and urbanised areas is also affecting water availability, quantity and quality. Buildings, roads, roofs, paved areas and other hard surfaces prevent rainfall from infiltrating into the soil, thus exacerbating flooding risks. Urban catchments in African cities often face significant land development pressures for agriculture or urban settlements (Figure 3.5). Water security can be at risk when cities are relying exclusively on surface water sources for their water supply, like in Cape Town, South Africa, for instance. It may also generate important additional investment costs to safeguard or augment water supply sources.

Figure 3.5. Land use in a selection of African cities

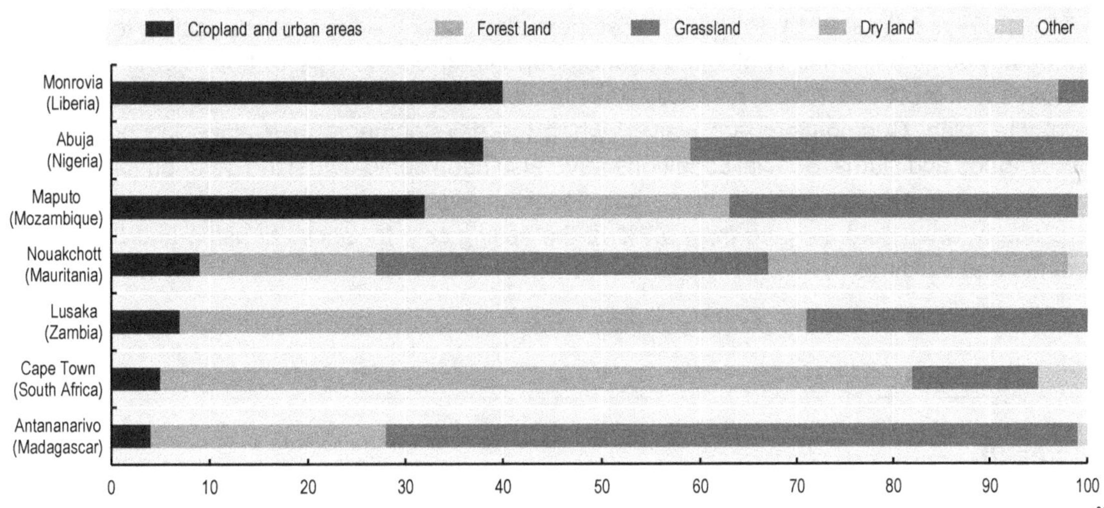

Source: The Nature Conservancy (2016[7]), *Sub-Saharan Africa's Urban Water Blueprint: Securing Water Through Water Funds and Other Investments in Ecological Infrastructure.* The Nature Conservancy, Nairobi.

Land use modification also alters species and their habitats. In Eastern Africa, the conversion of natural landscapes into cropland and livestock grazing resulted in soil modification affecting native plant species, which induced a reduction in the number and diversity of wildlife (The Nature Conservancy, 2016[7]). The unplanned urbanisation of African cities is also impeding further the development and implementation of coherent environmental and ecosystem conservation policies that could reduce water risks.

Acknowledging the influence of land use policy upon urban water policy, some cities set up tools to ensure better cross-sectoral policy coherence at the local level (Box 3.3). Nevertheless, most African cities are often struggling with overlapping and contradictory property systems, in which rights are often unclear and administrative systems function poorly. In Western Africa, for example, only 2%-3% of land is held with a government registered title. In several cases, the lack of coherence across sectoral policies has impeded the implementation of social measures to promote water access. In Abidjan, Côte d'Ivoire, for instance, a 75% subsidy was offered to low-income households for their first piped connection to the formal water supply. However, households had to provide proof of legal settlement; hence, the poor living in unplanned urban areas were usually not eligible for the subsidy (Ainuson, 2010[8]). In addition, across the continent, planning regulations are often anachronistic, restrictive and impracticable from an enforcement point of view (Lall, Henderson and Venables, 2017[9]).

Box 3.3. Land development taxes' contribution to network extension and social connections in Casablanca, Morocco

Casablanca is characterised by rapid urbanisation: its population is expected to grow from 3.5 million to 5 million by 2030. Extending the water network, securing access to the resource and protecting it against frequent floods are serious concerns for the local authority, which needs to finance these projects. The city defined a new investment programme in 2007 and contracted Lydec, a subsidiary of Suez Environnement, to provide water supply and sanitation (WSS) services and mitigate flood risks. Revenues from user tariffs cover operational and maintenance costs and the renewal of existing assets (accounting for 70% of total cost over the last decade). A dedicated account (*fonds de travaux*) covers the remaining costs (essentially land acquisition, network extension and social connections). Financed mainly by contributions from property developers, it has financed a growing share of total investment, from 7% in 2004 to 54% in 2014. Property developers also cover the costs of connecting to the network and inhouse equipment. Their contribution varies depending on the type of housing (social housing, villas, hotels and industrial zones) and they pay additional costs for developments that do not feature in the master plan. Contributions are waived when the developments take place in underprivileged neighbourhoods and slums. Special conditions have also been set to adjust the contribution to the pace of urban expansion and to harness major urban developments. The contribution is a share of the price of the property when sold, ranging from 0.7% of the selling cost for social housing to 1.3% for luxury apartments and buildings.

Source: OECD (2015[10]), *Water Resources Governance in Brazil*, https://doi.org/10.1787/9789264238121-en.

Public health

The interactions between public health policy and urban water management are also strong, as the COVID-19 pandemic showed (see Chapter 1). Contaminated water and poor sanitation are linked to the transmission of diseases such as cholera, diarrhoea, dysentery, hepatitis A, typhoid and polio. Microbiological contamination of groundwater and water-related diseases challenging for sub-Saharan Africa with low-income groups and children being disproportionately affected (Howard G, 2006[11]). The lack of access to clean water, sanitation and handwashing facilities is a leading to the death of some 842 000 people each year from diarrhoea, including 361 000 children aged under 5 each year (WHO Africa, 2021[12]). Faecal waste is the largest source of contamination in urban groundwater, in particular where there is high-density housing with poor and/or inadequate sanitation facilities and treatment. Water cuts and shortages in African cities also require households to switch temporarily from their principal water supply source to an alternative one, whether improved or not. This potentially generates varying social and health impacts on users, depending on the context (Santos et al., 2017[13]). The Kampala Water and Sanitation Forum (KWSF) facilitate co-ordination of stakeholders in developing an integrated water sanitation and hygiene (WASH) sector to develop and support the citywide integrated hygiene education/promotion strategy for upscaling public health and environmental management in Kampala (Box 3.4).

Box 3.4. Kampala Water and Sanitation Forum (KWSF): Supporting an integrated WASH sector

The overall objective of the KWSF is to streamline co-ordination of stakeholders in developing an integrated WASH sector through the identification of challenges, resources and opportunities for synergy and learning networks. It builds on existing and emerging innovations to enhance sustainable interventions to achieve total sanitation and universal access to clean and safe water targets in Kampala City. The strategic objectives of KWSF include:

- Develop a network for WASH actors to optimise co-ordination of planning, implementation and efficient resource allocation.
- Develop and support a citywide integrated hygiene education/promotion strategy for up-scaling public health and environmental management.
- Identify and streamline standards for appropriate technologies and operational guidelines for faecal sludge management.

- Provide a citywide strategic framework to operationalise and enforce public and household sanitation legal guidelines.
- Support citywide co-ordination of WASH infrastructure development, operation and maintenance.
- Enhance capacity building and knowledge management of the city WASH sector.

Source: KCCA (n.d.[14]), *Kampala Water and Sanitation Forum*, https://www.kcca.go.ug/Water%20and%20Sanitation%20Forum.

Solid waste management

Solid waste management also has a great impact on urban water management. With collection rates below 50% in many African cities (Table 3.1), unmanaged urban waste is increasing water risks. Indeed, this low level of service and the common lack of guidelines for the management of sanitary landfills are affecting water quality, generating runoff pollution into rivers and coastal waters. The lack of waste management also leads to blocked waterways which exacerbate flood and health risks (Lall, Henderson and Venables, 2017[9]). The situation is especially problematic in informal settlements where garbage piles up along walkways and roads, and in gutters, drains and waterways.

Table 3.1. Percent of municipal solid waste collected in selected African cities

Cities	Solid waste collection coverage (%)	Year
Lome	42	2002
Abidjan	30-40	2002
Dakar	30-40	2003
Nouakchott	20-30	2005
Lusaka	18	2005

Source: Lall, S., J. Henderson and A. Venables (2017[9]), *Africa's Cities: Opening Doors to the World*, World Bank, Washington, DC.

Improving water-related data, monitoring and evaluation

Understanding water systems that get more and more complex in a rapidly changing environment is a huge challenge that water managers have to face. Continuous monitoring of water systems and processes therefore appears crucial. As stated by the UN, "Data is the lifeblood of decision-making and the raw material for accountability. Quality and timely data are vital for enabling governments, international organisations, civil society, the private sector and the general public to make informed decisions and to ensure the accountability of representative bodies" (n.d.[15]). Data and data-related analytics make it possible to understand complex water systems from a holistic perspective. Nevertheless, an increasing number of institutions face a widening gap between emerging realities (like growing populations, climate change and rapid digitalisation) and their existing practices and capacities.

The GLAAS report 2019 provides information with regard to monitoring and evaluation practices of SDG 6 in African countries. In 34% of African countries (15 countries), regulatory authorities do not release publicly accessible reports on drinking water quality. The proportion reduces to 16% of countries (7 countries) for reports on treated wastewater flows and faecal sludge volumes (Figure 3.6). In all remaining countries, information is either partially published, not published or absent.

OECD Water Governance Principle n°5 on Data and Information

Produce, update and share timely, consistent, comparable and policy-relevant water and water-related data and information, and use it to guide, assess and improve water policy, through:

1. Defining requirements for cost-effective and sustainable production and methods for sharing high-quality water and water-related data and information, e.g. on the status of water resources, water financing, environmental needs, socio-economic features and institutional mapping.
2. Fostering effective co-ordination and experience sharing among organisations and agencies producing water-related data between data producers and users, and across levels of government.
3. Promoting engagement with stakeholders in the design and implementation of water information systems and providing guidance on how such information should be shared to foster transparency, trust and comparability (e.g. data banks, reports, maps, diagrams, observatories).
4. Encouraging the design of harmonised and consistent information systems at the basin scale, including in the case of transboundary water, to foster mutual confidence, reciprocity and comparability within the framework of agreements between riparian countries.
5. Reviewing data collection, use, sharing and dissemination to identify overlaps and synergies and track unnecessary data overload.

Source: OECD (2015[1]), *OECD Principles on Water Governance*, https://www.oecd.org/gov/regional-policy/OECD-Principles-on-Water-Governancebrochure.pdf.

OECD Water Governance Principle n°12 on Monitoring and Evaluation

Promote regular monitoring and evaluation of water policy and governance where appropriate, share the results with the public and make adjustments when needed, through:

1. Promoting dedicated institutions for monitoring and evaluation that are endowed with sufficient capacity, an appropriate degree of independence and resources as well as the necessary instruments.
2. Developing reliable monitoring and reporting mechanisms to effectively guide decision-making.
3. Assessing to what extent water policy fulfils the intended outcomes and water governance frameworks are fit for purpose.
4. Encouraging timely and transparent sharing of the evaluation results and adapting strategies as new information becomes available.

Source: OECD (2015[1]), *OECD Principles on Water Governance*, https://www.oecd.org/gov/regional-policy/OECD-Principles-on-Water-Governancebrochure.pdf.

Figure 3.6. Drinking water quality and treated wastewater flows and faecal sludge volumes, 2018/19

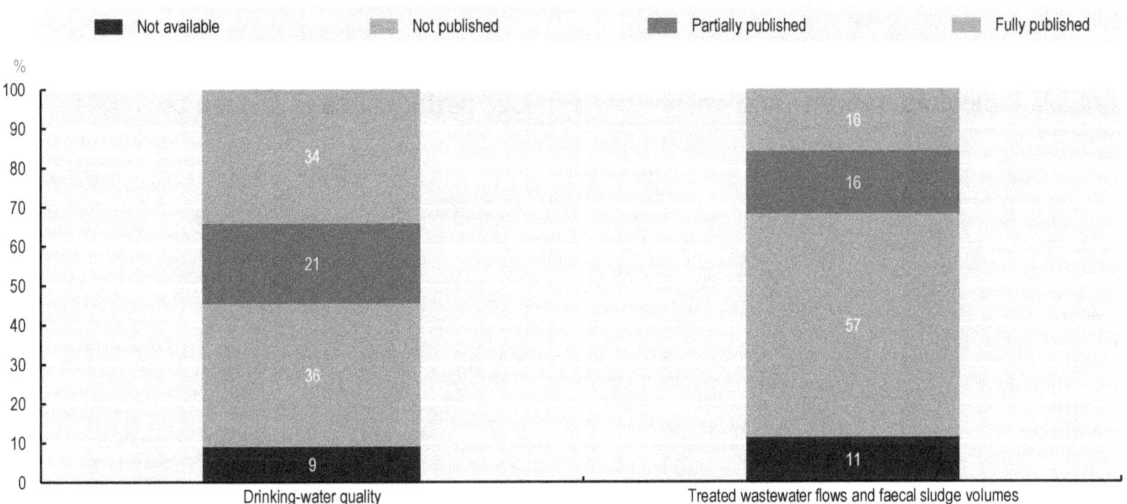

Note: Sample of 44 African countries.
Source: UN-Water (2019[16]), *National Systems to Support Drinking-water, Sanitation and Hygiene – Global Status Report 2019*; UN-Water (2019[17]), *Global Analysis and Assessment of Sanitation and Drinking-Water (GLAAS) 2019 Report.*

Data regarding the frequency of drinking water and sanitation surveillance against requirement also shows that much progress still needs to be made in Africa, as 27 countries do not monitor drinking water quality according to frequency requirements while 11 countries did not set any surveillance frequency requirements at all. Data for sanitation describe a similar situation with 20 countries not fulfilling monitoring frequency requirements while 18 countries did not set any surveillance frequency requirements at all (Figure 3.7). This situation is likely to generate issues with regard to the accuracy, the consistency and comparability of data, which can finally result in not being policy-relevant.

Figure 3.7. Frequency of surveillance in practice compared to requirements, 2018/19

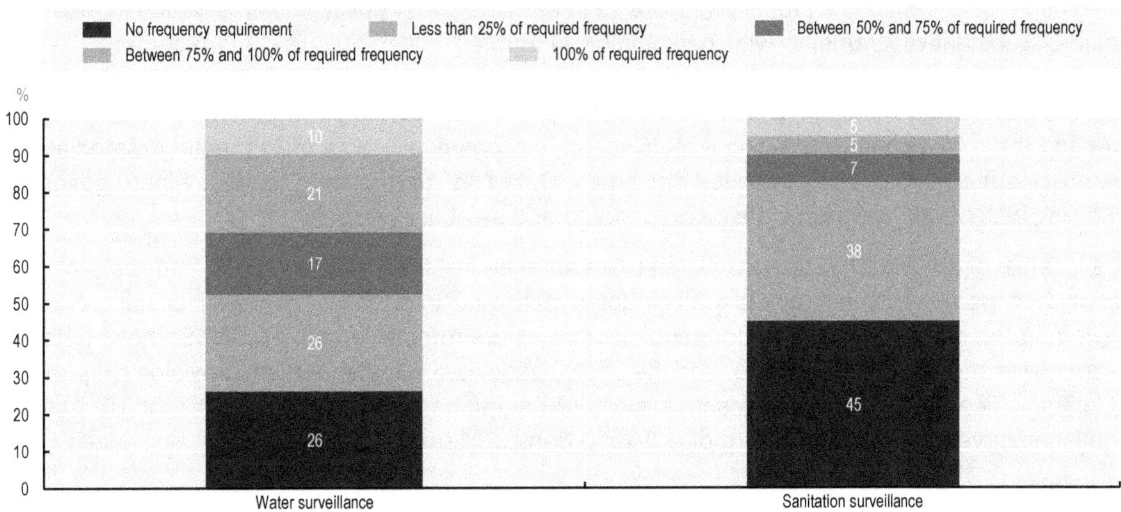

Note: Sample of 42 African countries for water surveillance and 40 countries for sanitation surveillance.
Source: UN-Water (2019[16]), *National Systems to Support Drinking-water, Sanitation and Hygiene – Global Status Report 2019*; UN-Water (2019[17]), *Global Analysis and Assessment of Sanitation and Drinking-Water (GLAAS) 2019 Report.*

The GLAAS report shows encouraging results with regard to the use of performance indicators, especially for water quality. However, much progress is still needed for treated effluent quality and sanitation (Figure 3.8).

Figure 3.8. Indicators on water and wastewater services performance in African countries, 2018/19

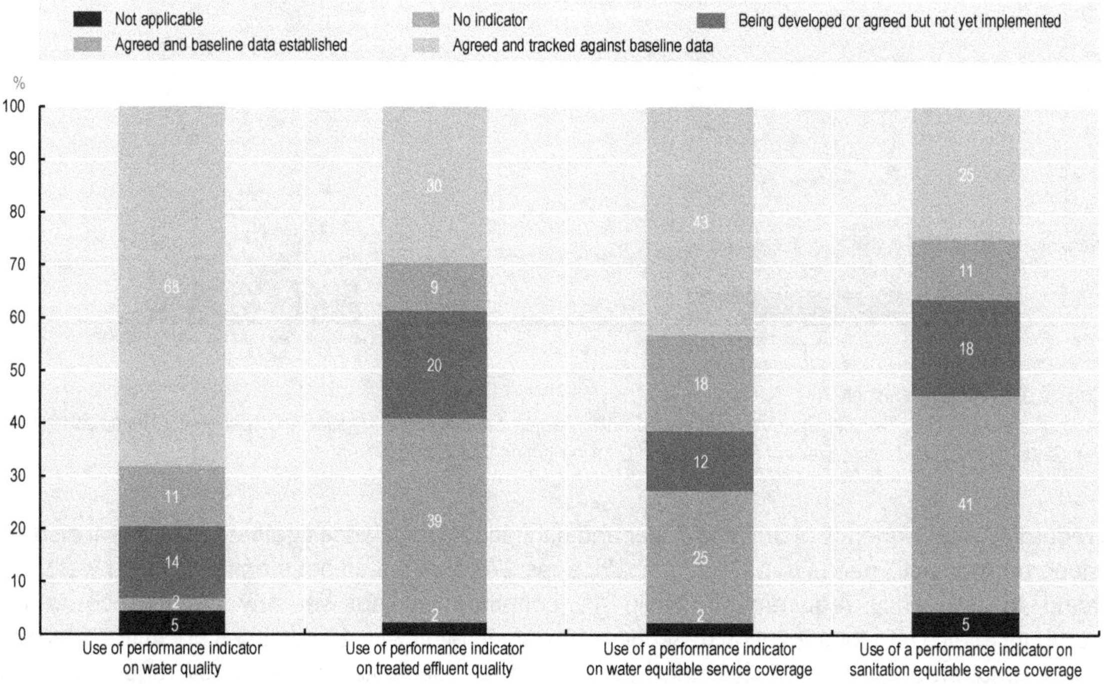

Note: Sample of 44 African countries.

Source: UN-Water (2019[16]), *National Systems to Support Drinking-water, Sanitation and Hygiene – Global Status Report 2019*; UN-Water (2019[17]), *Global Analysis and Assessment of Sanitation and Drinking-Water (GLAAS) 2019 Report*.

Missing information remains a prominent obstacle to effective water policy implementation in most African countries. Substantive problems with data inhibit integrated water resource management (IWRM) as mentioned in the first section of Chapter 3. This lack of data and information is further hampering any water policy evaluation and monitoring. The absence of periodical review and scrutiny of water policies is preventing the assessment of policies effectiveness and potentially from implementing remedial actions when policies are not delivering intended outcomes. Data and information gaps also hinder governments from taking water policy decisions based on updated and reliable evidence.

At the local level, the OECD Survey on Water Governance in African Cities (2021[6]) shows a contrasted situation with partial and incomplete water-related data and information available in half of the cities surveyed. In the other half, WSS performance indicators are routinely used. For WSS, these data mainly concern water and wastewater quality, and the costs associated with the service provision (Figure 3.9). In the Central African Republic, for instance, the city of Bangui has access to the data produced as part of the national survey on municipalities' profile (World Bank, 2017[18]).

Figure 3.9. Availability of local data on water and sanitation services in surveyed cities

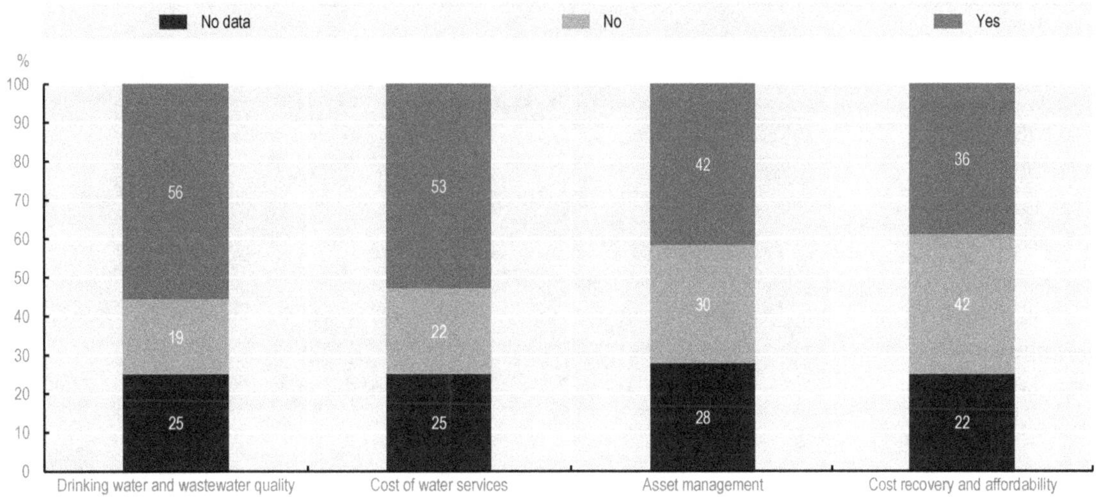

Note: 36 cities responded to the question 'Are the following data on city water and sanitation services available in your city?".
Source: OECD (2021[6]), *OECD Survey on Water Governance in African Cities*, OECD, Paris.

These results (Table 3.2) underline that most surveyed cities have some data available (more on water and wastewater quality than on cost recovery and affordability, for instance) which can be used to guide their WSS urban policy decision-making. In addition, in 61% of the surveyed cities, water and sanitation utilities are using performance indicators to monitor the quality and performance of WSS provision. This information is generally published yearly in reports available to the public (Table 3.3 and Table 3.4).

Table 3.2. Data on water and sanitation services in surveyed cities

Cities	Drinking water and wastewater quality	Cost of water services	Cost recovery and affordability	Asset management	Use of performance indicators
Abidjan (Côte d'Ivoire)					
Fes (Morocco)					
Al Hoceima (Morocco)					
Kampala (Uganda)					
Brazzaville (Republic of the Congo)					
Rabat (Morocco)					
Bobo-Dioulasso (Burkina Faso)					
Chefchaouen (Morocco)					
Rosso (Mauritania)					
Vogan (Togo)					
Meknes (Morocco)					
Tanger (Morocco)					
Lusaka (Zambia)					
Tetouan (Morocco)					
Cape Town (South Africa)					
Bangui (Central African Republic)					
Antananarivo (Madagascar)					

Cities	Drinking water and wastewater quality	Cost of water services	Cost recovery and affordability	Asset management	Use of performance indicators
Cotonou (Benin)	Yes	No	Yes	No	Yes
Thies (Senegal)	Yes	No answer	Yes	Yes	No
Bangangte (Cameroon)	Yes	No	No	Yes	Yes
Saint-Louis (Senegal)	No	Yes	No	Yes	Yes
Nouakchott (Mauritania)	No	Yes	No	No	Yes
Dionaba (Mauritania)	No	No	Yes	No	No
Banjul (Gambia)	No	No	Yes	No	No answer
Kanembakache (Niger)	No	No	No	No	Yes
Cocody (Côte d'Ivoire)	No	No	No	No	No
Monrovia (Liberia)	No	No	No	No	No answer
Golf 3 (Togo)	No answer	No	No	No	No
Accra (Ghana)	No answer	No answer	No answer	No answer	Yes
Marrakech (Morocco)	No answer	No answer	No answer	No answer	No
Mbour (Senegal)	No answer	No answer	No answer	No answer	No
Dakar (Senegal)	No answer	No answer	No answer	No answer	No
Maputo (Mozambique)	No answer	No answer	No answer	No answer	No answer
Lome (Togo)	No answer	No answer	No answer	No answer	No answer
Bama (Burkina Faso)	No answer	No answer	No answer	No answer	No answer
Abuja (Nigeria)	No answer	No answer	No answer	No answer	No answer

Note: 36 cities responded to the question "Are the following data on city water and sanitation services available in your city?".

Yes

No

No answer

Source: OECD (2021[6]), *OECD Survey on Water Governance in African Cities*, OECD, Paris.

Table 3.3. Using performance indicators to monitor service quality in Lusaka Zambia

Service indicator	Primary indicator	Service level
Coverage of service area	Percentage of population served with drinking water	88%
Drinking water quality	a. No. of tests carried out (bacteriological and residue chlorine)	According to NWASCO water quality guideline
	b. Percentage of results meeting the standard	95%
Service hours	a. Average daily water supply duration at connection	22 hours
	b. Average daily water supply duration at public distribution system	12 hours
	c. Office hours and pay point per week	40 hours
Billing for services	a. Frequency of billing customers	Once a month
	b. Frequency of customer meter reading	Once a month
	c. Payment period after bill delivered	2 weeks
	d. Percentage metering	75%
Client contact	a. Response time to written complaints	5 working days
	b. Response time for new connection	10 working days
	c. Response time for meter installation request	10 working days
	d. Response time for meter testing	10 working days
	e. Waiting time to pay bill or file complaint	15 minutes

Service indicator	Primary indicator	Service level
	f. Telephone contact holding time	5 minutes
Interruption of water supply and blockage of sewer	*Water* a. Percentage connected property subjected to unannounced supply interruption for 20-36 hours	< 15%
	b. 36-48 hours	< 5%
	c. Above 48	< 3%
	Sewer d. Percentage connected property subjected to sewer blockage 20-36 hours	< 10%
	e. 36-48 hours	< 8%
	f. More than 48 hours	< 3%
Pressure in the network for water supply	Connection with flow rate of fewer than 7 litres/minute	< 5% of connections in particular service area
Unjustified disconnection	Percentage of connections subjected to unjustified disconnection in a year	< 0.2%
Sewer flooding	Percentage of connections subjected to sewer flooding	< 0.3% of connections in particular service area
Quality of discharged sewer	a. No. of tests carried out (bacteriological and chemical)	According to ZEMA licence conditions
	b. Percentage of results meeting ZEMA standard	40% for bacteriological and 60% for chemical

Source: Lusaka Water and Sewerage Company (2015[19]), *Service Level Guarantee 2015-2018.*

Table 3.4. National Water and Sewerage Corporation performance monitoring, Uganda

Category	Fiscal year 2018/19	Fiscal year 2017/18
Economic sustainability		
Turnover (UGX thousand)	442 000 000	388 000 000
Operating expenditure (UGX thousand)	346 000 000	296 000 000
Operating profits (UGX thousand)	96 000 000	92 000 000
Investment made (UGX thousand)	302 000 000	258 000 000
Asset base (UGX thousand)	3 100 000 000	1 700 000 000
Number of towns	253	236
Environmental and ecological sustainability		
Number of towns using solar pumps	25	22
Number of towns using electrolysis instead of chlorination	25	25
Volume of sewerage treated and discharged (million litres)	100	95
Expenditure on energy (UGX billion)	66	57
Social sustainability		
Domestic customers served	535 532	479 729
Commercial/industrial customers served	88 340	78 761
Institutional/government customers served	17 368	17 368
Public Stand Post consumers served	17 186	13 728
Total number of customers served	659 157	587 863
Water mains extension (km)	2 727	2 171
Sewer mains extension (km)	59	24
Number of customer complaints received	166 698	147 708
Number of customer complaints handled	163 557	138 567
Resolution rate of complaints (%)	98	94

Category	Fiscal year 2018/19	Fiscal year 2017/18
Number of staff employed	3 778	3 443
Staff costs (UGX thousands)	137 265 190	112 000 000
New water connections	69 215	50 341
New sewer connections	368	272
Corporate social responsibility		
Amount spent on donations (UGX thousand)	914 000	1 300 000
Number of beneficiaries of donations	5 000 000	3 000 000
Amount paid in taxes (UGX thousand)	40 000 000	38 000 000
Human resource sustainability		
Number of staff recruited	355	310
Number of employees over 55 years	119	117
Total number of staff + Board	3 778	3 443
Gender composition (staff + board)	Female 30 Male 70	Female 29 Male 71
Amount spent in long time awards (UGX thousand)	57 000	120 000
Amount spent on research and training (UGX thousand)	750 000	700 000
Number of interns trained	1 700	1 500

Source: NWSC (2019[20]), *Integrated Annual Report 2018/2019*, National Water and Sewerage Corporation.

With regard to water resource management, half of the surveyed cities produce or have access to data regarding water abstractions, water-related disasters and meteorological information at the city level (Figure 3.10).

Figure 3.10. Available local data on water risk management in surveyed African cities

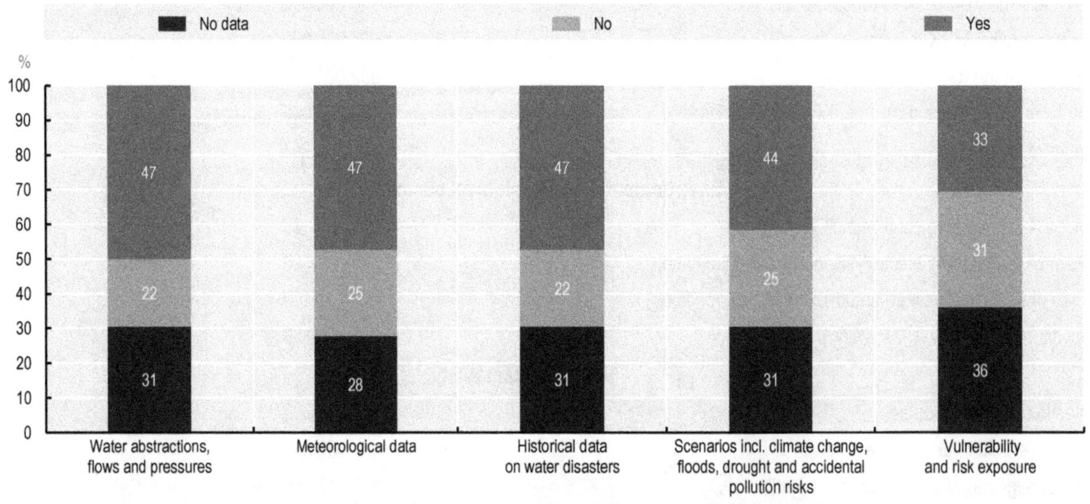

Note: 36 cities responded to the question "Are the following data on risk management available at the local level for your city?".
Source: OECD (2021[6]), *OECD Survey on Water Governance in African Cities*, OECD, Paris.

In one-third of the surveyed African cities, key data on water resources management are produced regularly at the city level (Table 3.5). When these data exist, they are often part of a harmonised, integrated, standardised and co-ordinated information system across the country. However, the survey shows that such data are not frequently publicly available and communicated to users (only one out four times). In addition, missing and patchy information stemming from incomplete, outdated and/or fragmented data, remains a prominent obstacle to effective water policy implementation, evaluation and monitoring in most cities surveyed.

Table 3.5. Data on water risk management in surveyed cities

Cities	Water abstractions	Meteorological data	Historical data on water disasters	Scenarios incl. climate change, floods, drought & pollution risks	Vulnerability & risk exposure
Kanembakache (Niger)	Yes	Yes	Yes	Yes	Yes
Tanger (Morocco)	Yes	Yes	Yes	Yes	Yes
Rabat (Morocco)	Yes	Yes	Yes	Yes	Yes
Marrakech (Morocco)	Yes	Yes	Yes	Yes	Yes
Lusaka (Zambia)	Yes	Yes	Yes	Yes	Yes
Cotonou (Benin)	Yes	Yes	Yes	Yes	Yes
Tetouan (Morocco)	Yes	Yes	Yes	Yes	Yes
Saint-Louis (Senegal)	Yes	Yes	Yes	Yes	Yes
Thies (Senegal)	Yes	Yes	Yes	Yes	Yes
Cape Town (South Africa)	Yes	Yes	Yes	Yes	No
Chefchaouen (Morocco)	Yes	Yes	Yes	Yes	No answer
Abidjan (Côte d'Ivoire)	Yes	Yes	Yes	No answer	Yes
Fes (Morocco)	Yes	Yes	Yes	No	No
Golf 3 (Togo)	Yes	Yes	Yes	No	No
Brazzaville (Republic of the Congo)	Yes	Yes	Yes	No	No
Bangangte (Cameroon)	Yes	No	Yes	Yes	Yes
Kampala (Uganda)	Yes	No	Yes	No answer	No
Nouakchott (Mauritania)	No	No	No	Yes	Yes
Bangui (Central African Republic)	No answer	Yes	No answer	Yes	No answer
Vogan (Togo)	No	Yes	No	No	No
Banjul (Gambia)	No	No	No	Yes	No
Antananarivo (Madagascar)	No answer	No answer	No answer	Yes	No answer
Meknes (Morocco)	No	No	No	No	No
Al Hoceima (Morocco)	No	No	No	No	No answer
Monrovia (Liberia)	No	No	No	No	No
Cocody (Côte d'Ivoire)	No	No	No	No	No
Dionaba (Mauritania)	No	No	No	No	No
Accra (Ghana)	No answer	No answer	No answer	No answer	No answer
Maputo (Mozambique)	No answer	No answer	No answer	No answer	No answer
Lome (Togo)	No answer	No answer	No answer	No answer	No answer
Mbour (Senegal)	No answer	No answer	No answer	No answer	No answer
Dakar (Senegal)	No answer	No answer	No answer	No answer	No answer
Bobo-Dioulasso (Burkina Faso)	No answer	No answer	No answer	No answer	No answer
Bama (Burkina Faso)	No answer	No answer	No answer	No answer	No answer
Rosso (Mauritania)	No answer	No answer	No answer	No answer	No answer
Abuja (Nigeria)	No answer	No answer	No answer	No answer	No answer

Note: 36 cities responded to the question "Are the following data on risk management available at the local level for your city?".
Yes
No
No answer
Source: OECD (2021[6]), *OECD Survey on Water Governance in African Cities*, OECD, Paris.

Addressing the funding gap

According to SDG 6 monitoring, 27% of the sub-Saharan population use a safely managed drinking water service and 18% a safely managed sanitation service (UN-Water, 2017[21]). In sub-Saharan urban areas, this proportion reaches 50% for water and 20% for sanitation. Hence considerable investment efforts are still required to achieve SDG 6.1.1 and 6.2.1 targets by 2030. Furthermore, among the 25 African countries reporting in the GLAAS report 2019 (UN-Water, 2019[17]) on national systems to support drinking water, sanitation and hygiene, 20 declared that the financing allocated to sanitation improvements correspond to less than 50% of what is actually needed to meet national targets.

The OECD Council (OECD, 2016[22]) recommends setting up measures for the sustainable financing of water services, water infrastructures, water resources management and protection of water-related ecosystems by:

1. Considering the following four principles for financing water resources management: "polluter pays", "beneficiary pays", equity and coherence between policies that affect water resources.
2. Aiming for the greatest social returns to investment, for example through:
    - Exploring options that can minimise current or future financing needs while addressing trade-offs and exploiting synergies between policy objectives and between short- and long-term challenges.
    - Taking stock of existing assets, maintaining them, looking for efficiency gains.
    - Developing strategic financial plans that match financial resources with policy objectives and ensuring affordability for vulnerable segments of society, including through ad hoc targeted measures.
    - Setting up an independent review of the efficiency and cost-effectiveness of investments.
3. Considering diversifying revenue streams and tapping into new sources of capital, where needed and in line with policy objectives. A first step could be to combine revenues from water tariffs, transfers from public budgets and transfers from the international community to recover the costs of investment, operation and maintenance of water infrastructure as much as possible and where efficient.

OECD Water Governance Principle n°6 on the Governance-financing Nexus

Ensure that governance arrangements help mobilise water finance and allocate financial resources in an efficient, transparent and timely manner, through:

1. Promoting governance arrangements that help water institutions across levels of government raise the necessary revenues to meet their mandates, building through principles such as the "polluter pays" and "user pays" principles, for example, as well as payment for environmental services.
2. Carrying out sector reviews and strategic financial planning to assess short-, medium- and long-term investment and operational needs and take measures to help ensure availability and sustainability of such finance.
3. Adopting sound and transparent practices for budgeting and accounting that provide a clear picture of water activities and any associated contingent liabilities including infrastructure

investment, and aligning multi-annual strategic plans to annual budgets and medium-term priorities of governments.

4. Adopting mechanisms that foster the efficient and transparent allocation of water-related public funds (e.g. through social contracts, scorecards, and audits).
5. Minimising unnecessary administrative burdens related to public expenditure while preserving fiduciary and fiscal safeguards.

Source: OECD (2015[1]), *OECD Principles on Water Governance*, https://www.oecd.org/gov/regional-policy/OECD-Principles-on-Water-Governancebrochure.pdf.

The OECD makes a distinction between the three ultimate sources of finance for water-related investments (revenues from tariffs, taxes and transfers from the international community) and other sources of repayable finance (loans, bonds, etc.) (Figure 3.11). Taxes and tariffs are very important for not only raising revenue but also for demand management and signalling the value of water, water services and water security.

Figure 3.11. Potential sources of funding and financing for water-related investments

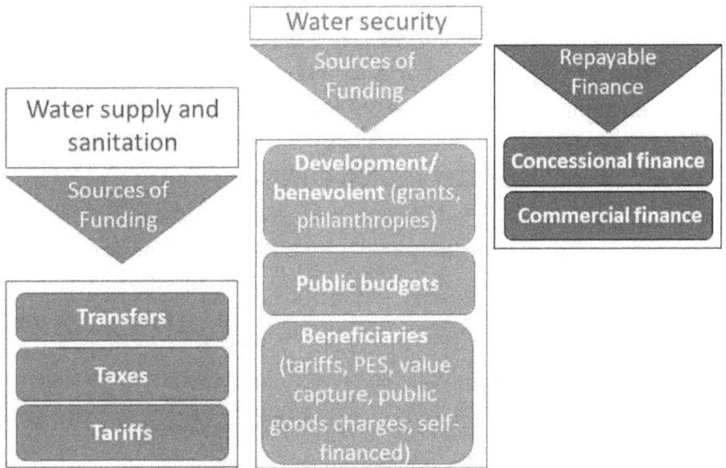

Source: Adapted from OECD (2010[23]), *Innovative Financing Mechanisms for the Water Sector*, https://doi.org/10.1787/9789264083660-en.

Repayable sources of finance require a creditworthy borrower, which can provide a financial return. Notably, there is a growing consensus that mobilising commercial finance (through blended finance or other means, such as a combination of equity and debt) will be instrumental to achieve the SDGs and provide the incentives to put the water sectors' financing on a more sustainable footing. Bearing in mind the megatrends that affect African countries, achieving the SDGs for water and sanitation throughout the African continent will require consistent investment in water infrastructure, operations and maintenance, efficient management of water resources, and strengthened policy and regulatory frameworks. Current annual total spending in the region represents USD 8-13 billion (Figure 3.12). Compared to the estimated annual need of USD 22 billion (USD 15 billon capital expenditure and USD 7 billion for operations and maintenance), the yearly expenditure fulfils between 34% and 60% of the projected needs (ICA, 2019[24]).

Figure 3.12. Total water sector financing sources in Africa, 2013-18

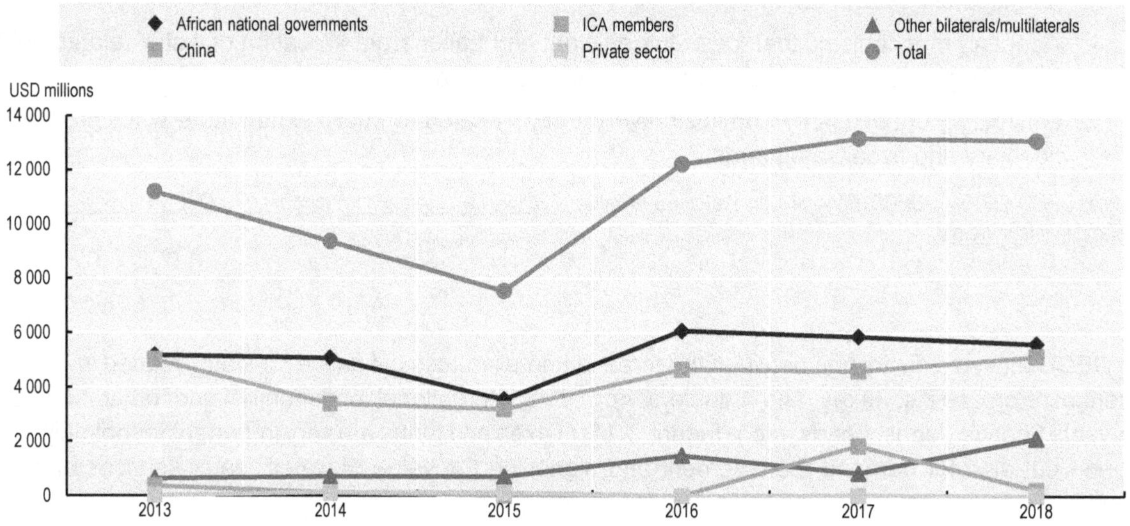

Note: The complete list of ICA members is available on ICA website: https://www.icafrica.org/fr/about-ica/ica-members/.
Source: ICA (2019[24]), *About ICA*, https://www.icafrica.org/fr/about-ica/ica-members/.

Furthermore, it is estimated that the annual costs required addressing issues related to access to sanitation, access to drinking water, water resource management and water scarcity represent 1.44% of the African continent gross domestic product (GDP) (Figure 3.13).

Figure 3.13. Annual costs required per water-related challenge for the African continent, % of GDP

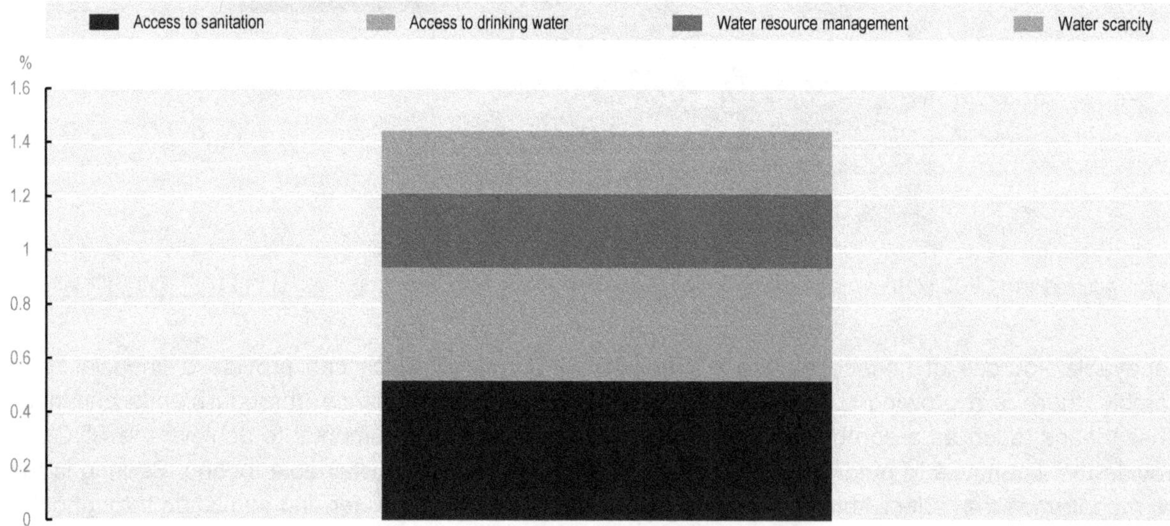

Source: Strong, C. et al. (2020[25]), "Achieving abundance: Understanding the cost of a sustainable water future", Working Paper, World Resources Institute, Washington, DC, www.wri.org/publication/achieving-abundance.

When solely focusing on investment, Eastern Africa, which represents one-third of the total African population, accounted for the largest share (31%) of new investment in the water and sanitation sector across Africa. Northern Africa accounted for 20% while representing 18% of the African inhabitants. The Republic of South Africa accounted for 18%, while Southern Africa (5% of the African population) and

Western Africa (30% of the African population) accounted for 12%. Only 7% of new funding for water and sanitation was invested in Central Africa (representing 13% of the continent's population) (Figure 3.14).

Figure 3.14. Share of total water and sanitation investment by African region, 2018

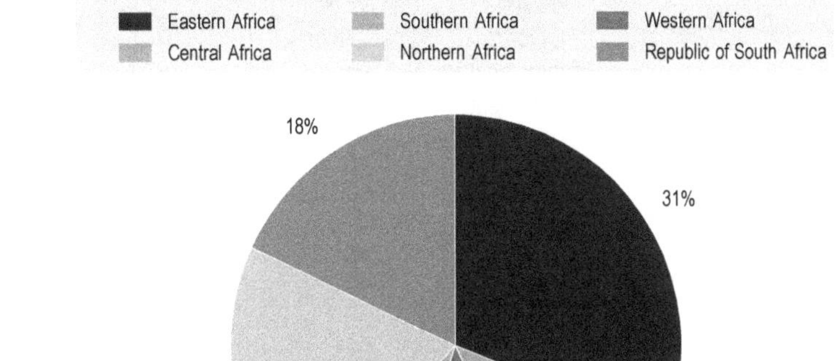

Source: ICA (2019[24]), *About ICA*, https://www.icafrica.org/fr/about-ica/ica-members/.

National governments in Africa need to dramatically increase the amounts of public funding invested in WASH services. Official development assistance, although critical is insufficient. It can, however, help leverage investments from other sources, such as commercial and blended finance, including from the private sector. A certain proportion of the investment gap could also be covered through increased efficiency with technical losses representing from 20% to 50%, and collection ratio ranging from 80% to 95% throughout Africa (IBNet, n.d.[26]). Subsidies and tariff structures must also be appropriately designed, targeted and implemented with the objectives to achieve sustainability, equity, affordability and the appropriate level of service for all.

Confirming the existing funding gap, all surveyed African cities declare that lack of funding is the first obstacle to good water governance and is also the first water-related priority for the future. Surveyed cities also note that the ageing, obsolete or absence of infrastructure is another major challenge that they have to face especially in a context of rapid urbanisation and population growth. Indeed, long-lasting underinvestment has jeopardised the development and provision of needed urban water infrastructure. Thus, all surveyed cities declare that building, operating and maintaining WSS infrastructure is a top priority on their agenda.

Tariffs and subsidies are the most commonly used funding sources for utilities. A total of 70% of the cities surveyed state that formal urban water services are resorting to tariffs and subsidies (Table 3.6) and about half of the cities surveyed use transfers as a funding source for their water services. It should be noted that 44% of the respondent cities have set up cross-subsidy schemes through the implementation of a differentiated water tariff for industrial or large consumers. A total of 58% of the cities surveyed use tariffs as a funding source for formal urban sanitation services, while half of the cities declare that subsidies are also an important source of financing. Both for water and sanitation, official development assistance (ODA) is a funding source that is less resorted to by cities (in number not in volume).

Table 3.6. Financing sources of urban water and sanitation services in surveyed cities

Cities	Water supply			Sanitation		
	Tariffs	Subsidies from the central, regional and/or local government	Financial transfer from international aid	Tariffs	Subsidies from the central, regional and/or local government	Financial transfer from international aid
Abidjan (Côte d'Ivoire)	Yes	Yes	Yes	Yes	Yes	Yes
Fes (Morocco)	Yes	Yes	Yes	Yes	Yes	Yes
Kampala (Uganda)	Yes	Yes	Yes	Yes	Yes	Yes
Cotonou (Benin)	Yes	Yes	Yes	Yes	Yes	Yes
Thies (Senegal)	Yes	Yes	Yes	Yes	Yes	Yes
Vogan (Togo)	Yes	Yes	Yes	Yes	No	Yes
Bangangte (Cameroon)	Yes	Yes	Yes	Yes	No	Yes
Brazzaville (Republic of the Congo)	Yes	Yes	Yes	Yes	No	No
Bama (Burkina Faso)	Yes	Yes	Yes	No	No	Yes
Bangui (Central African Republic)	Yes	Yes	Yes	No answer	No answer	No answer
Nouakchott (Mauritania)	Yes	Yes	Yes	No answer	No answer	No answer
Dionaba (Mauritania)	Yes	Yes	Yes	No answer	No answer	No answer
Saint-Louis (Senegal)	Yes	Yes	No	Yes	Yes	Yes
Meknes (Morocco)	Yes	Yes	No	Yes	Yes	No
Al Hoceima (Morocco)	Yes	Yes	No	Yes	Yes	No
Tanger (Morocco)	Yes	Yes	No	Yes	Yes	No
Rabat (Morocco)	Yes	Yes	No	Yes	Yes	No
Cape Town (South Africa)	Yes	Yes	No	Yes	Yes	No
Mbour (Senegal)	Yes	Yes	No answer	Yes	Yes	No answer
Golf 3 (Togo)	Yes	No	Yes	Yes	Yes	Yes
Lusaka (Zambia)	Yes	No	Yes	Yes	No	Yes
Kanembakache (Niger)	Yes	No answer	Yes	No	Yes	Yes
Marrakech (Morocco)	Yes	No answer	No answer	Yes	No answer	No answer
Tetouan (Morocco)	Yes	No	No	Yes	No	No
Bobo-Dioulasso (Burkina Faso)	Yes	No	No	Yes	No	No
Monrovia (Liberia)	No	Yes	Yes	Yes	Yes	Yes
Cocody (Côte d'Ivoire)	No	Yes	Yes	No	Yes	Yes
Antananarivo (Madagascar)	No answer	Yes	Yes	No answer	No answer	Yes
Rosso (Mauritania)	No	Yes	Yes	No answer	No answer	No answer
Chefchaouen (Morocco)	No	Yes	No	No	Yes	No
Banjul (Gambia)	No	Yes	No	No	Yes	No
Accra (Ghana)	No answer	No answer	No answer	No answer	No answer	No answer
Maputo (Mozambique)	No answer	No answer	No answer	No answer	No answer	No answer
Lome (Togo)	No answer	No answer	No answer	No answer	No answer	No answer
Dakar (Senegal)	No answer	No answer	No answer	No answer	No answer	No answer
Abuja (Nigeria)	No answer	No answer	No answer	No answer	No answer	No answer

Note: 36 respondent cities to the question "in your city, through which funding source are the water supply and sanitation services financed?".
Yes
No
No answer
Source: OECD (2021[6]), *OECD Survey on Water Governance in African Cities*, OECD, Paris.

In Africa, water tariff setting is mostly driven at the national level either by a national service provider, a line ministry or a national regulator. As a result, 79% of the surveyed cities state that they do not make decisions over water tariff setting as there is uniform national guidance. This is, for instance, the case in Morocco where a ministerial decision is providing the specifications for water tariff setting or in Ghana where the Public Utility Regulatory Commission is setting the tariff policy.

Some countries, like Côte d'Ivoire, as part of their centralised tariff setting policy, have established the operating cost recovery principle as a rule for urban WSS. Operating costs of urban WSS must be covered by revenues from the water sales without resorting to resources from the central state budget. In addition, two earmarked funds financed via the water invoice have been set up, namely the National Water Fund and the Development Fund. The former ensures the repayment of loans contracted for the benefit of the water supply and sanitation sector while the latter finances social connections, works to renew installations, works to strengthen and extend the network, and invests in works.

Water abstraction and pollution charges are another economic instrument that can help manage resources through partially reflecting some of the costs associated with using or polluting it. These charges can be used to fund the costs of managing water resources and regulating activities that impact water availability and quality. The general principle for setting water abstraction or pollution charges is to reflect the externalities that related actions by one user cause to third parties and the environment. However, this task requires an important capacity to produce, update and share consistent and comparable data and information on the state of environment and resources, and to carry out technical and socio-economic assessments.

While pollution and abstraction charges are often driven by national regulatory and policy frameworks, there are not common in all African countries and cities. Abstraction charges are being collected in 58% of the cities surveyed, whereas pollution charges are less developed (36%) (Table 3.7). Reasons for the slower uptake of pollution charges in the management of water pollution may include: political resistance from polluters; limited data on the costs of environmental degradation; difficulties in measuring sources of pollution and attributing them to polluters.

Table 3.7. Economic instruments for water resources management in surveyed cities

Cities	Water abstraction charges	Water pollution charges
Abidjan (Côte d'Ivoire)		
Marrakech (Morocco)		
Cape Town (South Africa)		
Kampala (Uganda)		
Lusaka (Zambia)		
Antananarivo (Madagascar)		
Golf 3 (Togo)		
Saint-Louis (Senegal)		
Thies (Senegal)		
Dakar (Senegal)		
Brazzaville (Republic of the Congo)		
Bobo-Dioulasso (Burkina Faso)		
Rosso (Mauritania)		
Vogan (Togo)		
Meknes (Morocco)		
Al Hoceima (Morocco)		
Fes (Morocco)		

Cities	Water abstraction charges	Water pollution charges
Rabat (Morocco)	Yes	No
Bangangte (Cameroon)	Yes	No
Monrovia (Liberia)	Yes	No
Chefchaouen (Morocco)	Yes	No answer
Nouakchott (Mauritania)	No	No
Tanger (Morocco)	No	No
Cotonou (Benin)	No	No
Tetouan (Morocco)	No	No
Cocody (Côte d'Ivoire)	No	No
Banjul (Gambia)	No	No
Kanembakache (Niger)	No answer	No
Dionaba (Mauritania)	No answer	No
Accra (Ghana)	No answer	No answer
Maputo (Mozambique)	No answer	No answer
Lome (Togo)	No answer	No answer
Bangui (Central African Republic)	No answer	No answer
Mbour (Senegal)	No answer	No answer
Bama (Burkina Faso)	No answer	No answer
Abuja (Nigeria)	No answer	No answer

Note: 36 cities responded to the question "Which of the following economic instruments are in place for water management in your city?".
Yes
No
No answer
Source: OECD (2021[6]), *OECD Survey on Water Governance in African Cities*, OECD, Paris.

The absence, low level or low enforcement of economic instruments to manage water resources in African cities can represent a threat to water security in the region. For instance, although charges for water resource management and waste discharge exist in South Africa, they are set too low to serve as an effective economic instrument to manage water resources. Indeed, economic tools could be used to force water users and polluters to internalise the economic consequences of their water abstraction/pollution and encourage a behavioural change, and to fund the costs of managing water resources and regulating activities that impact water availability and quality.

Addressing transparency and integrity issues

Water infrastructure is typically capital-intensive and long-lived with high sunk costs, which exposes the sector to important corruption risks unless sound integrity, transparency and procurement frameworks are in place across the national and local levels. Water infrastructure calls for a high initial investment mainly funded through public expenditure (see the previous section) and procurement. Public procurement represents on average 13% to 20% of world GDP. Global expenditure in procurement is estimated at nearly USD 9.5 trillion throughout the world (World Bank, 2021[27]) and, according to the UN Office on Drugs and Crime, 10% to 25% of a public contract's overall value may be lost due to corruption (UNODC, 2013[28]).

Mainstreaming integrity and transparency practices across water policies, water institutions and water governance frameworks are key for greater accountability and trust in decision-making, and effective implementation of water policies. A low level of adoption of integrity tools can be a major threat to water security as investments can be discouraged by widespread corruption practices, despite considerable needs. For instance, this can prevent the increase in water and sanitation coverage thus hindering the potential for economic development, health and hygiene improvement, or ecosystems preservation. According to the UN Global Programme Against Corruption (UNDP, 2011[29]), corruption emphasises water scarcity threat by undermining government institutions, increasing the gap between rich and poor, and fostering illicit behaviours, which in turn threatens social and political stability and triggers violence. Whereas the magnitude of corruption varies substantially between countries and across areas of the water sector, the World Bank (World Bank, 2006[30]) has assessed that 20% to 40% of the water sector finances are being lost to dishonest practices.

OECD Water Governance Principle n°9 on Integrity and Transparency

Mainstream integrity and transparency practices across water policies, water institutions and water governance frameworks for greater accountability and trust in decision-making, through:

1. Promoting legal and institutional frameworks that hold decision-makers and stakeholders accountable, such as the right to information and independent authorities to investigate water-related issues and law enforcement.
2. Encouraging norms, codes of conduct or charters on integrity and transparency in national or local contexts and monitoring their implementation.
3. Establishing clear accountability and control mechanisms for transparent water policymaking and implementation.
4. Diagnosing and mapping, on a regular basis, existing or potential drivers of corruption and risks in all water-related institutions at different levels, including for public procurement.
5. Adopting multi-stakeholder approaches, dedicated tools and action plans to identify and address water integrity and transparency gaps (e.g. integrity scans/pacts, risk analysis, social witnesses).

Source: OECD (2015[1]), *OECD Principles on Water Governance*, https://www.oecd.org/gov/regional-policy/OECD-Principles-on-Water-Governancebrochure.pdf.

Corruption remains a prevalent issue in Africa as sub-Saharan Africa is the lowest-scoring region of Transparency International's annual Corruption Perceptions Index, with many of the region's countries among the worst-performing, although Botswana, Cabo Verde and the Seychelles rank among the top 25% worldwide (Transparency International, 2020[31]). However, there is a large diversity of situations across the continent with most Northern African countries in the top two-thirds performing countries, (with the exception of Libya) as well as Rwanda.

The water sector is no exception to corruption in Africa: 20% of respondents from 34 African countries having tried to obtain utility services (water, sanitation and electricity) claimed to have paid some form of bribe between 2016 and 2018, and over half of the respondents said that their governments were "failing" them in the provision of clean water and sanitation services (Howard, 2020[32]).

The diverse forms of corruption and integrity failures in the water sector have a wide range of consequences: they increase costs, lead to poor delivery outcomes and undermine social trust. Reducing costs and promoting trust is essential; especially in the context of a pandemic like COVID-19 where public resources are under pressure and the stakes of non-compliance with government recommendations are high. Because it is hidden from public view, corruption is difficult to quantify but some estimates are available: for example, research from Kenya suggests that corruption may have accounted for at least 4% of total public WASH expenditure in 2015/16 (Water Integrity Network, forthcoming[33]).

Promoting transparency and integrity in the water sector in Africa is crucial to ensure efficient, cost-effective and fair access to water and sanitation. The OECD Survey on Water Governance in African Cities (2021[6]) highlights the ongoing efforts to adopt integrity and transparency tools at the city level. For instance, in 58% of the surveyed cities, water accounts are separated from city accounts thus ensuring a clear identification of water-related revenues and spending. However, these efforts need to be strengthened. Less than half of the surveyed cities declare that clear procurement processes or clear budget transparency principles are duly applied. Only one-third of the surveyed cities have annual disclosure of financial information of water and sanitation services, or random audits, or anti-bribery management systems (Table 3.8).

Table 3.8. Transparency and integrity mechanisms in surveyed cities

	Water budget auditing	Water financial information disclosure	Budget transparency principles applied	Anti-bribery management systems	Whistle-blower protection policies	Anti-corruption plans, integrity charters	Clear procurement processes	Random audits	Prevention of conflict of interest
Kanembakache (Niger)									
Al Hoceima (Morocco)									
Bangangte (Cameroon)									
Tetouan (Morocco)									
Meknes (Morocco)									
Tanger (Morocco)									
Cotonou (Benin)									
Lusaka (Zambia)									
Cape Town (South Africa)									
Kampala (Uganda)									
Accra (Ghana)									
Antananarivo (Madagascar)									
Chefchaouen (Morocco)									
Thies (Senegal)									
Fes (Morocco)									
Vogan (Togo)									
Golf 3 (Togo)									
Brazzaville (Republic of the Congo)									
Dionaba (Mauritania)									
Rosso (Mauritania)									
Bama (Burkina Faso)									
Nouakchott (Mauritania)									

	Water budget auditing	Water financial information disclosure	Budget transparency principles applied	Anti-bribery management systems	Whistle-blower protection policies	Anti-corruption plans, integrity charters	Clear procurement processes	Random audits	Prevention of conflict of interest
Mbour (Senegal)									
Saint-Louis (Senegal)									
Bobo-Dioulasso (Burkina Faso)									
Banjul (Gambia)									
Cocody (Cote d'Ivoire)									
Marrakech (Morocco)									
Bangui (Central African Republic)									
Maputo (Mozambique)									
Monrovia (Liberia)									
Lome (Togo)									
Rabat (Morocco)									
Abuja (Nigeria)									
Dakar (Senegal)									
Abidjan (Cote d'Ivoire)									

Note: 36 cities responded to the question "Which mechanisms have been put in place at the city level to enhance transparency and integrity for water-related issues management?".

Yes

No

No answer

Source: OECD (2021[6]), *OECD Survey on Water Governance in African Cities*, OECD, Paris.

Strengthening stakeholder engagement

In a rapidly changing and connected world where climate change, population growth, urban development, rising water need for energy and food, natural disasters and water risks are likely to damage societies and the environment, stakeholders must be empowered to act together to shape water governance. Stakeholders that compose the water sector play a crucial role in determining the outcome of a given policy or project. They can initiate and support it, but they can also oppose efforts, attempt to block them or divert them to serve their own aims. Stakeholder engagement provides opportunities to share objectives, experiences and responsibilities, and to secure more support to the solutions that will be reached while voicing and addressing concerns and interests. As such, stakeholder engagement is a means for groups and individuals to share tasks and responsibilities in a sector where they often contribute to challenges as well as solutions.

OECD Water Governance Principle n°10 on Stakeholder Engagement

Promote stakeholder engagement for informed and outcome-oriented contributions to water policy design and implementation, through:

1. Mapping public, private and non-profit actors who have a stake in the outcome or who are likely to be affected by water-related decisions, as well as their responsibilities, core motivations and interactions.
2. Paying special attention to under-represented categories (youth, the poor, women, Indigenous peoples, domestic users), newcomers (property developers, institutional investors) and other water-related stakeholders and institutions.
3. Defining the line of decision-making and the expected use of stakeholders' inputs, and mitigating power imbalances and risks of consultation capture from over-represented or overly vocal categories, as well as between expert and non-expert voices.
4. Encouraging capacity development of relevant stakeholders as well as accurate, timely and reliable information, as appropriate.
5. Assessing the process and outcomes of stakeholder engagement to learn, adjust and improve accordingly, including the evaluation of costs and benefits of engagement processes.
6. Promoting legal and institutional frameworks, organisational structures and responsible authorities that are conducive to stakeholder engagement, taking account of local circumstances, needs and capacities.
7. Customising the type and level of stakeholder engagement to the needs and keeping the process flexible to adapt to changing circumstances.

Source: OECD (2015[1]), *OECD Principles on Water Governance*, https://www.oecd.org/gov/regional-policy/OECD-Principles-on-Water-Governancebrochure.pdf.

The reporting of SDG 6.b.1 on "stakeholder participation" shows that two-thirds of African countries have defined procedures in law or policy for the participation of local communities in water and sanitation planning. On the contrary, only one-third of African countries have developed such participation procedures for water resource planning and management (Figure 3.15).

Figure 3.15. Legal provisions for local communities' participation in water and sanitation planning, in Africa (SDG 6.b.1)

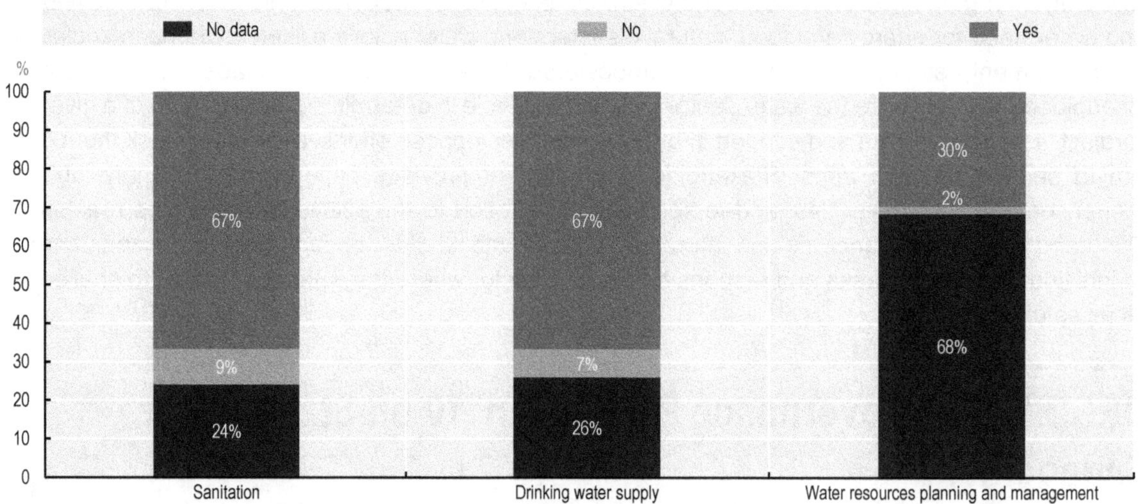

Note: 54 African countries.
Source: UN-Water (2019[16]), *National Systems to Support Drinking-water, Sanitation and Hygiene – Global Status Report 2019*; UN-Water (2019[17]), *Global Analysis and Assessment of Sanitation and Drinking-Water (GLAAS) 2019 Report*.

Furthermore, the extent of local community participation for water and sanitation planning remains moderate to low in urban areas throughout the African continent, thus highlighting the need to improve effective stakeholder engagement (Figure 3.16). This finding is compounded by insufficient financial resources, which hamper the implementation of community participation procedures. Over 85% of countries in sub-Saharan Africa report that financial resources were less than 50% of that needed to support community participation in 2017 (UN-Water, 2019[17]).

Figure 3.16. Local community participation in water and sanitation planning in urban areas in Africa (SDG 6.b.1)

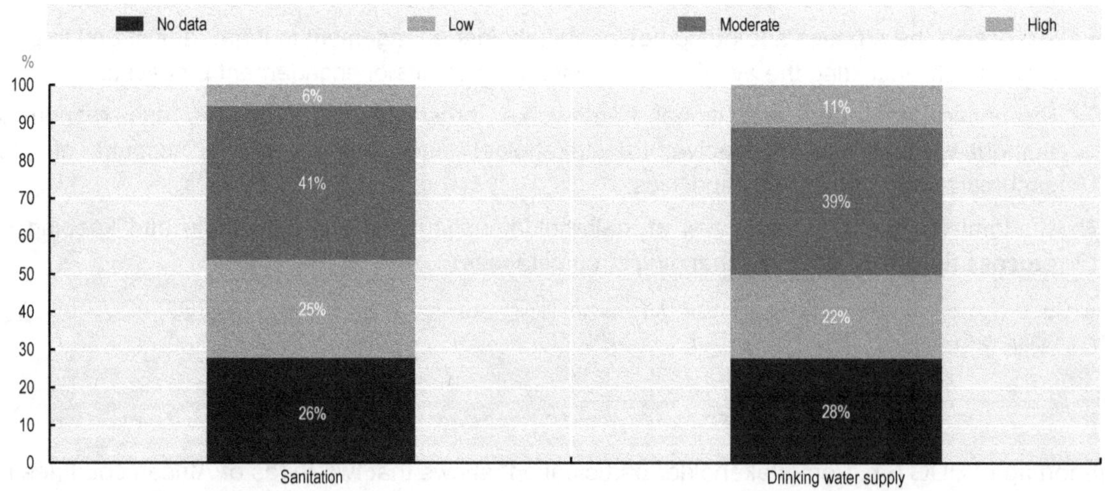

Note: 54 African countries.
Source: UN-Water (2019[16]), *National Systems to Support Drinking-water, Sanitation and Hygiene – Global Status Report 2019*; UN-Water (2019[17]), *Global Analysis and Assessment of Sanitation and Drinking-Water (GLAAS) 2019 Report*.

These findings are confirmed by the results of the OECD Survey on Water Governance in African Cities (2021[6]), where most respondents declare facing obstacles to engaging stakeholders in water-related matters. The lack of funding, time and staff along with the complexity of the issues at hand or the low capacity of stakeholders to engage in consultation processes represent some of these impediments. The political discontinuity and the weak legal framework to support engagement are also reported as significant issues (Figure 3.17). In such a context, cities believe that improving knowledge, information and competency will be key to strengthen stakeholder engagement and citizen awareness on water-related topics in the future. For instance, in August 2017, the city of Cape Town established a Water Resilience Advisory Committee (WRAC) as a response to the drought crisis in order to gather a variety of stakeholders outside the municipal administration and foster information and knowledge. In its 2019 Water Strategy (City of Cape Town, 2019[34]), Cape Town capitalised on this experience to further create a Collaborative Resilience Action Plan - a multi-stakeholder platform to co-ordinate efforts and improve governance and decision-making during any crisis.

Figure 3.17. Main obstacles to stakeholder engagement in surveyed African cities

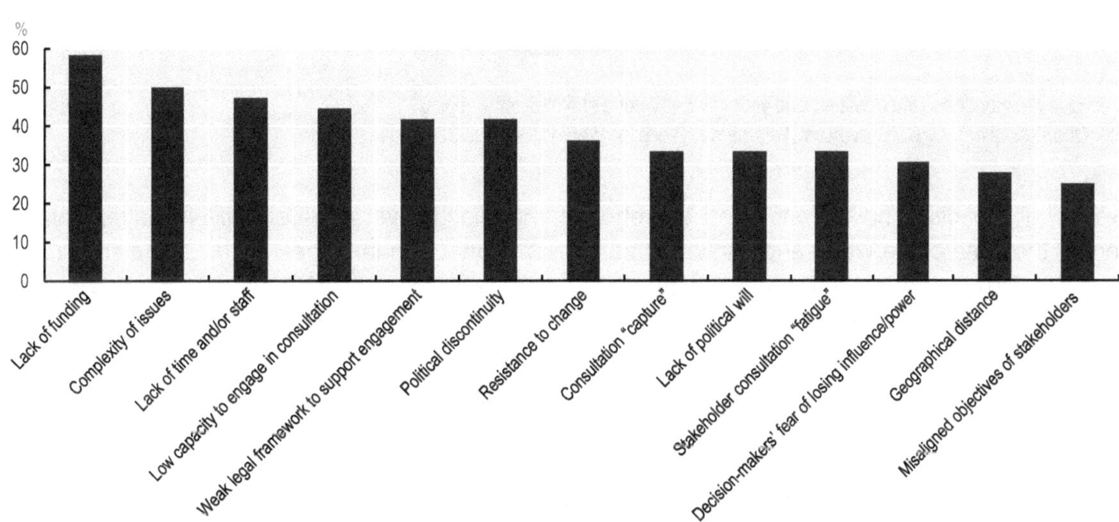

Note: 32 cities responded to the question "Which obstacles mostly hinder stakeholder engagement in your city?".
Source: OECD (2021[6]), *OECD Survey on Water Governance in African Cities*, OECD, Paris.

In addition to the above-mentioned obstacles, African cities also declare that some categories of stakeholders are more difficult to engage with than others. Service providers (28%) and central government (28%) are reported as the most difficult counterparts to engage with, followed by vulnerable groups (19%). In response, 42% of cities have implemented specific mechanisms for poor populations and population living in informal settlements. For instance, in Accra, the Ghana Water Company Limited established a unique Low-Income Customer Support Unit (LICSU) to exclusively deal with unserved areas in the country. The LICSU ensures that newly developed and unserved urban settlements are piped and connected to the network. This unit provides affordable and sustainable solutions to increase access to safely managed drinking water for the urban poor. In 2019, the unit successfully managed to connect almost 10 000 low-income households to piped water supply.

Besides the difficulties encountered to engage with stakeholders, African cities are primarily lacking basic knowledge about the stakeholders they should engage with. More than three surveyed cities out of four have not carried out a stakeholder mapping for their water sector (Figure 3.18). Such mapping allows to clearly identify public, private and non-profit actors that have a stake in the outcome or that are likely to be affected by water-related decisions, as well as their responsibilities, core motivations and interactions. This mapping can be considered as a first step to guide and build stakeholder engagement processes.

Figure 3.18. Share of surveyed cities that have carried out a water-related stakeholder mapping

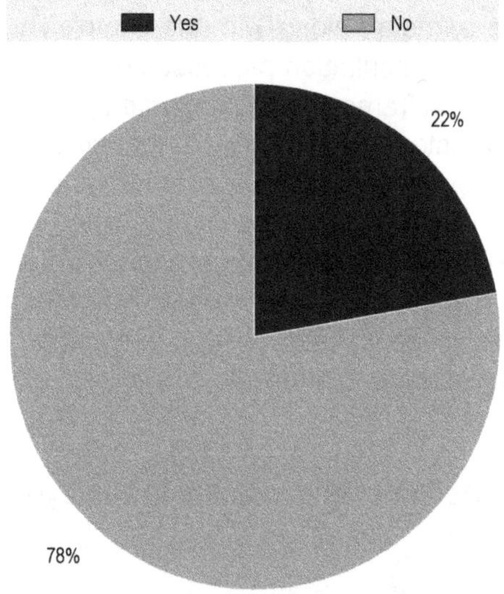

Note: 33 cities responded to the question "Did your city carry out a stakeholder mapping?".
Source: OECD (2021[6]), *OECD Survey on Water Governance in African Cities*, OECD, Paris.

However, if few cities have conducted stakeholder mapping, several water utilities have. This is, for instance, the case of the water and sanitation service provider Lyonnaise des Eaux Casablanca (LYDEC) in Morocco (Box 3.5) or of the National Water and Sewerage Corporation (NWSC) in Uganda (Box 3.6). In both cases, utilities also resort to specific engagement mechanisms.

Box 3.5. LYDEC stakeholder mapping and engagement in Casablanca, Morocco

The development of a responsible dialogue with stakeholders is a structuring axis of LYDEC Corporate Social Responsibility strategy, through a dedicated strategic project, adopted in January 2016 by the general management. Detailed mapping of stakeholders was carried out and validated by the Sustainable Development Steering Committee on 14 April 2016. This was followed by an exercise of prioritisation of these stakeholders with regard to three critical elements: power, urgency and legitimacy. The mapping confirms the existence of a complex ecosystem of stakeholders, made of two main categories:

- Internal stakeholders including employees, governance bodies, social partners, etc.
- External stakeholders comprising regulators, economic partners and societal influencers.

Table 3.9. List of existing engagement mechanisms with stakeholders in Casablanca, Morocco

Stakeholders	Description	Engagement mechanisms
Internal stakeholders	• Customers: Individual consumers, professionals, administrations and communities, industries • Water and electricity suppliers • Subcontractors • Promoters/developers • Banks/investors	• Meetings of the General Management Committee, Strategic Projects Monitoring Committee, Board of Directors • Internal blog • Internal campaigns (including service commitments, innovation, security, sustainable development and business projects) • Communication on our sites (safety) • Guides (welcome, good behaviour, etc.) • Management report (shareholders)

Regulators	• Delegating authority • Supervisory authority • Regulatory authorities • Professional federations and associations • Certification/labelling bodies	• Delegated Management Monitoring Committee • Regular meetings with the Permanent Control Service of the Delegating Authority, the Management of *Régies* and licensed services, etc. • Lydec website • Activity report • Delegated management report (authorities) • Onsite visits • Project presentation brochures (Eaucéan station, etc.)
Economic partners	• Governance bodies (Board of Directors, General Management Committee) • Social partners • Shareholders (Suez, RMA, Fipar Holding…) • Lydec employees • Lydec Foundation	• Customer relations centre • Lydec website, social networks and external blog • Publications ("Lydec & Vous") and posting in branches, in the service areas and publications distributed in the branch network • 2016 image review • Annual general public satisfaction survey • Activity report • Meetings and visits to suppliers and subcontractors
Societal influencers	• Elected officials and local authorities/councils, districts and municipalities • Media and social networks • Associations and non-governmental organisations (NGOs) • Civil society • Financial and extra-financial analysts/rating agencies • Universities/research	• Proximity meetings with elected officials and local authorities • Lydec pages on social networks • Actions of the Lydec Foundation • 2016 image review • Visits to worksites and brochures (Eaucéan gallery, Médiouna experimental space, Le 7/24 Lydec monitoring and co-ordination centre, etc.) • Annual media seminar and press releases (media)

Source: Lyonnaise des Eaux Casablanca, (2016[35]) *Rapport de contribution sociale, sociétale et environnementale.*

Box 3.6. Water-related stakeholder mapping and engagement in Uganda

The NWSC has a diverse range of stakeholders, including consumers, government, development partners, suppliers, employees and the community. While focusing on the implementation of water supply and sewerage services, the corporation takes into consideration the need to balance this mandate with the needs of all the stakeholders.

Engaging with stakeholders helps understand their dynamic expectations and strive to meet them. The stakeholders mapping is summarised in the table below.

Table 3.10. List of existing engagement mechanisms with stakeholders in Uganda

Stakeholders	Importance	Engagement mechanisms
Consumers	• Pay their bills • Consume our services • Give us feedback • Market our services • Support our growth	• Monthly meter readings and issuing of bills • Prompt communication on service interruptions • Annual update of customer charter • Annual customer satisfaction survey • Social media platform for customer interactions and engagements which include: NWSC website, Twitter, Facebook, WhatsApp, YouTube and Instagram

		• 24h toll-free call centre • Various payment options that are convenient to our customers, including: bank counters, direct debit, mobile money and NWSC application • 184 branch offices spread to various parts of the country • E-branch where customers can access various services such as new connections
Government	• Sole equity owner • Commitment to support the provision of universal access to water • Providing policy and regulatory framework	• Present budgets, work plans and strategies for approval • Make quarterly and annual reports to government • Participate in parliamentary committee meetings to present our plans, achievements and challenges • Working closely with other departments in the implementation of government programmes
Development partners	• Contribute funding to our capital development projects • Support capacity development programmes	• Provide work plans and reports on a quarterly basis • Participate in donor conferences to understand their changing priorities • Participate in project review meetings with the development partners
Employees	• They run the business • They interface with all other stakeholders • Possess the key skills required in our business	• Clear working terms and conditions of services • Written work instructions, health and safety guidelines • Regular meetings between staff and management • Laid down procedures for resolving conflicts • Staff social activities like sport, weekly breakfasts and training workshops • Bi-annual performance appraisals and reviews • Whistle-blower policy to encourage staff report wrongdoings • Coaching and mentoring with the management team • Regular visits to branch offices by management and board

Source: National Water and Sewerage Corporation, (2019[36]), *Integrated Annual Report 2018/19.*

Cities are using a variety of mechanisms to engage with water-related stakeholders (Figure 3.19). Meetings (56%) and workshops (44%) are the predominant engagement tools, followed by citizen committees (42%) and subnational water institutions such as river basin organisations (42%). In Cameroon, the city of Bangangté has set up a water and sanitation communal committee as a forum for discussion, decision-making and action relating to water and sanitation issues at the municipal level. The committee gathers water users as well as municipal officials. Its annual meeting is open to the public and chaired by the mayor. In Lusaka, Zambia, for instance, the Lusaka Water Security Initiative, a multi-stakeholder collaboration platform gathering stakeholders from all sectors, aims to foster dialogue, knowledge sharing, awareness raising, planning and project development in the view to improve water security (Box 3.7).

Box 3.7. Successful stakeholder engagement examples in Zambia

Lusaka Water Security Initiative (LuWSI)

Founded in 2016, LuWSI is a multi-stakeholder collaboration platform gathering over 20 partners from the public sector, private sector, civil society and international institutions. LuWSI partners engage in dialogue and leadership, analysis and knowledge sharing, advocacy and awareness raising, planning and project development with the objective of improving water security for the residents and businesses of Lusaka. LuWSI is not, as of yet, a registered legal entity but rather a voluntary partnership of partners, bound together through a memorandum of understanding (MoU).

LuWSI's core functions are to:

- Assess, prioritise and monitor water security threats and solutions.
- Create awareness, education and advocacy for change.
- Develop and implement projects; mobilise new actors and resources.
- Strengthen capacity for multi-stakeholder collaboration.

LuWSI has five water security action areas, prioritised by its partners during a series of strategy development workshops:

- Groundwater pollution prevention.
- Sustainable groundwater exploitation.
- Healthy Kafue River.
- Access to water supply and sanitation.
- Urban flood risk management.

Source: LuWSI (n.d.[37]), *Homepage*, https://www.luwsi.org/.

Water Watch Groups (WWGs)

In Zambia, the National Water and Sanitation Council (NWASCO), which regulates the water and sanitation sector, has a very lean structure with offices in Lusaka only. However, in wanting to ensure that NWASCO is present on the ground for first-hand information and addressing consumer complaints, WWGs have been established, comprising customers from the service areas. WWG functions include: representation of consumer interests; follow-up of unresolved consumer complaints; improvement of the communication between consumers and providers; arbitration in conflicts between consumers and service providers; collection of information on providers' performance; information of NWASCO on regulations effectiveness and the proposition of possible adjustments; information of poor consumers with regard to their rights and obligations; and information of consumers with regards to the role and functions of NAWSCO. To fulfil these functions, WWGs hold public meetings with consumers and meetings to review/validate complaints. They engage in outreach and publicity programmes via awareness meetings, television and radio broadcasts. They submit periodic reports to NWASCO including feedback from consumers. They participate in workshops, conferences, etc. They assist in the recruitment and training of new WWGs.

Source: NAWSCO (n.d.[38]), *Water Watch Groups*, http://www.nwasco.org.zm/index.php/consumer-service/water-watch-groups.

Figure 3.19. Stakeholder engagement mechanisms used by surveyed African cities

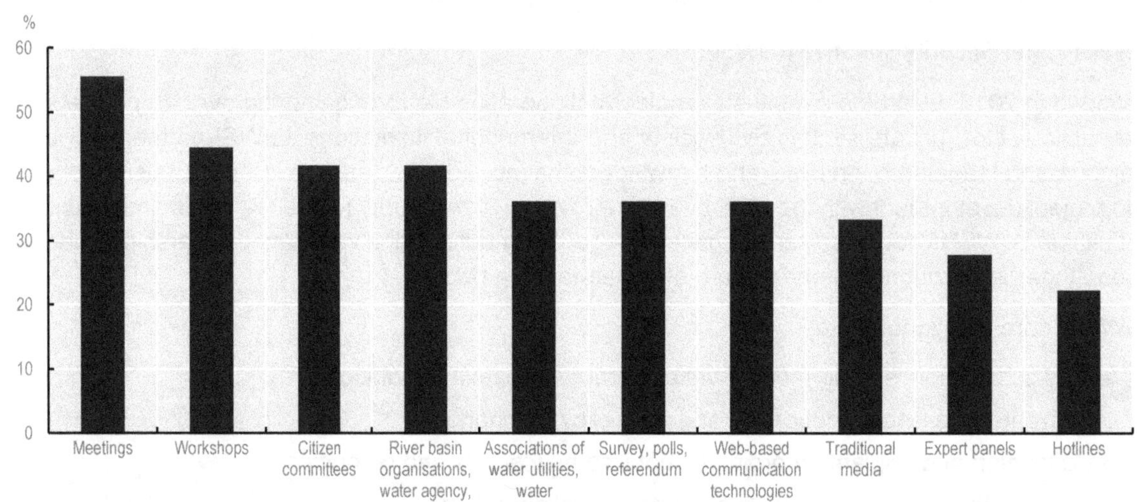

Note: 24 cities responded to the question "Which mechanisms does your city mostly use to engage stakeholders in water-related decision-making?".
Source: OECD (2021[6]), *OECD Survey on Water Governance in African Cities*, OECD, Paris.

In a tentative taxonomy, the OECD (2015[39]) describes some of the advantages and drawbacks that both formal and informal engagement mechanisms bring about.

- Formal mechanisms such as water associations and river basin organisations are often based on the principle of representative democracy, which confers them legitimacy. However, they can also be perceived as single-minded when they focus solely on pushing forward the agenda of a single group of stakeholders. River basin organisations can present challenges in terms of lobbying and consultation capture when discussions and decisions are "highjacked" or monopolised by the interests of certain groups. It can also generate principle-agent tensions by which the person sitting at the table voices his/her own concern rather than representing his/her broader constituency. This should be a key concern when selecting stakeholders to participate in advisory boards, working groups or assemblies.
- The relatively informal nature of meetings and workshops can foster both deliberation and build a sense of community. They provide an open atmosphere which makes participants generally more willing to discuss issues and maximises dialogues on issues that may not come to light through more structured mechanisms. For instance, meetings and workshops are flexible in terms of timeframe and scale (from community meetings to international conferences) and can apply to a wide range of issues (e.g. from discussing a municipal sewer project to debating on transboundary basin management agreements). They offer an opportunity for anyone to express concerns, access and share information, and gain a better understanding. However, if tools used to involve stakeholders do not have a minimal level of structure and mediation, outcomes may be difficult to incorporate into final decisions. Follow-up is also needed to turn views and concerns into actual contributions to decision-making beyond information sharing.

Critical aspects of governance should guide stakeholder engagement frameworks. Fair and equitable access to engagement opportunities is key to ensure a balanced and representative process that takes into account diverse ideas and opinions. Being transparent and open about the ways to identify stakeholders, choose engagement mechanisms and define the objectives pursued can help to raise interest among stakeholders and develop an understanding of and support for the final decisions. It is not sufficient to provide platforms for stakeholders to share their ideas as decision-makers must also clearly demonstrate how these ideas are taken into account. Procedural transparency and timely disclosure of information, including alternative solutions, are therefore critical to ensure the legitimacy of decision-making processes and their outcomes. Engagement processes may bring together groups with opposing views who fear that their views will not be taken into account. Showing participants what the intention of the process is and how their input will be considered is important to ensure productive discussions and exchange of opinions. It is also important that decision-makers be able to trust the quality and value of input from non-technical experts.

References

Ainuson, K. (2010), "Urban water politics and water security in disadvantaged urban communities in Ghana", *African Studies Quarterly*, Vol. 11/4, p. 59. [8]

AMCOW (2018), *Status Report on the Implementation of Integrated Water Resources Management in Africa: A Regional Report for SDG Indicator 6.5.1 on IWRM Implementation*. [3]

CICOS (n.d.), *Homepage*, International Commission for the Congo-Oubangui-Sangha Basin, https://www.cicos.int/. [4]

City of Cape Town (2019), *Cape Town Water Strategy*, Department of Water and Sanitation, http://resource.capetown.gov.za/documentcentre/Documents/City%20strategies%2c%20plans%20and%20frameworks/Cape%20Town%20Water%20Strategy.pdf. [34]

Global Water Partnership (2000), "No 4: Integrated water resources management", Technical Advisory Committee. [2]

Howard G, B. (2006), *Groundwater and public health*, World Health Organization, IWA Publishing, pp. 3-19. [11]

Howard, B. (2020), *African governments failing in provision of water and sanitation, majority of citizens say"*, https://afrobarometer.org/sites/default/files/publications/Dispatches/ab_r7_dispatchno349_pap14_water_and_sanitation_in_africa.pdf. [32]

IBNet (n.d.), *Homepage*, International Benchmarking Network, https://www.ib-net.org/ (accessed on 15 February 2021). [26]

ICA (2019), *About ICA*, Infrastructure Consortium for Africa, https://www.icafrica.org/fr/about-ica/. [24]

KCCA (n.d.), *Kampala Water and Sanitation Forum*, Kampala Capital City Authority, https://www.kcca.go.ug/Water%20and%20Sanitation%20Forum. [14]

Lall, S., J. Henderson and A. Venables (2017), *Africa's Cities: Opening Doors to the World*, World Bank, Washington, DC. [9]

Lusaka Water and Sewerage Company (2015), *Service Level Guarantee 2015-2018*. [19]

LuWSI (n.d.), *Homepage*, Lusaka Water Security Initiative, https://www.luwsi.org/ (accessed on 15 February 2021). [37]

Lyonnaise des Eaux Casablanca (2016), *Rapport de contribution sociale, sociétale et environnementale*. [35]

National Water and Sewerage Corporation (2019), *Integrated Annual Report, 2018/19.* [36]

NAWSCO (n.d.), *Water Watch Groups*, National Water and Sanitation Council, http://www.nwasco.org.zm/index.php/consumer-service/water-watch-groups. [38]

NWSC (2019), *Integrated Annual Report 2018/2019*, National Water and Sewerage Corporation. [20]

OECD (2021), *OECD Survey on Water Governance in African Cities*, OECD, Paris. [6]

OECD (2016), *OECD Council Recommendation on Water*, https://www.oecd.org/environment/resources/Council-Recommendation-on-water.pdf. [22]

OECD (2015), *OECD Principles on Water Governance*, OECD, Paris, https://www.oecd.org/gov/regional-policy/OECD-Principles-on-Water-Governancebrochure.pdf. [1]

OECD (2015), *Stakeholder Engagement for Inclusive Water Governance*, OECD Studies on Water, OECD Publishing, Paris, https://doi.org/10.1787/9789264231122-en. [39]

OECD (2015), *Water Resources Governance in Brazil*, OECD Studies on Water, OECD Publishing, Paris, https://doi.org/10.1787/9789264238121-en. [10]

OECD (2010), *Innovative Financing Mechanisms for the Water Sector*, OECD Studies on Water, OECD Publishing, Paris, https://doi.org/10.1787/9789264083660-en. [23]

OMVS (n.d.), *Homepage*, Organisation for the Development of the Senegal River, https://www.omvs.org/. [5]

Santos, S. et al. (2017), "Urban growth and water access in sub-Saharan Africa: Progress, challenges, and emerging research directions", *Science of the Total Environment*, Vol. 607-608, pp. 497-508. [13]

Strong, C. et al. (2020), "Achieving abundance: Understanding the cost of a sustainable water future", Working Paper, World Resources Institute, Washington, DC, http://www.wri.org/publication/achieving-abundance. [25]

The Nature Conservancy (2016), *Sub-Saharan Africa's Urban Water Blueprint: Securing Water Through Water Funds and Other Investments in Ecological Infrastructure*, The Nature Conservancy, Nairobi. [7]

Transparency International (2020), *Corruption Perceptions Index 2020*, https://images.transparencycdn.org/images/CPI2020_Report_EN_0802-WEB-1_2021-02-08-103053.pdf. [31]

UN (n.d.), *Big Data for Sustainable Development*, United Nations, https://www.un.org/en/sections/issues-depth/big-data-sustainable-development/index.html. [15]

UNDP (2011), *Fighting Corruption in the Water Sector. Methods, Tools and Good Practices*, https://www.undp.org/content/dam/undp/library/Democratic%20Governance/IP/Anticorruption%20Methods%20and%20Tools%20in%20Water%20Lo%20Res.pdf. [29]

UNODC (2013), *Guidebook on anti-corruption in public procurement*, https://www.unodc.org/documents/corruption/Publications/2013/Guidebook_on_anti-corruption_in_public_procurement_and_the_management_of_public_finances.pdf. [28]

UN-Water (2019), *Global Analysis and Assessment of Sanitation and Drinking-Water (GLAAS) 2019 Report*, United Nations. [17]

UN-Water (2019), *National Systems to Support Drinking-water, Sanitation and Hygiene – Global Status Report 2019*, United Nations. [16]

UN-Water (2017), *Sub-Saharan Africa*, United Nations, https://sdg6data.org/region/Sub-Saharan%20Africa. [21]

Water Integrity Network (forthcoming), *Water Integrity Global Outlook 2021*. [33]

WHO Africa (2021), *Water*, https://www.afro.who.int/health-topics/water. [12]

World Bank (2021), *Global Public Procurement Database: Share, Compare, Improve!*, https://www.worldbank.org/en/news/feature/2020/03/23/global-public-procurement-database-share-compare-improve. [27]

World Bank (2017), *République Centrafricaine, Enquête nationale sur les monographies communales 2016*. [18]

World Bank (2006), *The private sector side of the corruption equation. Independent commission against corruption (ICAC) Symposium*. [30]

Annex A. OECD Survey on Water Governance

OECD Survey questionnaire

1. Megatrends and water risks

1.1 Which of the following megatrends are putting water resources at risk in your city?
Climate change
Demographic changes (population migration or displacement, growth, etc.)
Urbanisation (sprawl, informal settlement growth, etc.)
Economic development and growth
Food insecurity (increasing water demand from the agricultural sector)
Global crisis/emergency-driven events (health shocks, political instability, armed conflicts, geopolitical unrest, etc.)

1.2 Which of the following challenges tend to drive the increase in water services coverage in your city?
Urbanisation (sprawl, informal settlement growth, etc.)
Demographic changes (population migration or displacement, growth, etc.)
Fighting poverty and social inequalities
Institutional and territorial reforms (decentralisation, aggregation and mergers of regions/provinces/municipalities)
Fighting waterborne diseases (malaria, dengue, etc.)

1.3 Where does the impetus to recognise the importance of water in your city mostly come from?
National laws, regulations and initiatives
Local mayor leadership and commitment
International donors, development agencies
Citizen pressure, civil society organisations
United Nations human right to water and sanitation, Sustainable Development Goals (SDGs) and/or Agenda 2030

1.4 Which of the following water risks are the most important in your city?
Too much water (floods)
Too little water (droughts)
Too polluted water (e.g. contaminated surface/groundwater sources)
Insufficient coverage of water and sanitation services
Ageing, obsolete infrastructure/Lack of infrastructure
Competition/conflicts over water allocation
Waterborne diseases (malaria, dengue, etc.)

1.5 Please describe more specifically 3 key water risks your city is presently facing, providing some key data and trends:

2. Institutions

2.1 Is your city in charge of the following responsibilities with regard to water and sanitation services?
If yes, please specify which ones:
Tariff regulation
Definition of quality standards for drinking water
Monitoring of quality standards for drinking water
Definition of quality standards for wastewater treatment
Monitoring of quality standards for wastewater treatment
Defining public service obligations
Defining technical/industry and service standards
Setting incentives for efficient use of water resources
Setting incentives for efficient investment
Information and data gathering
Monitoring of service delivery performance
Customer engagement
Consumer protection and dispute resolution
Licensing of municipal water operators
Supervision of contracts between utilities and private actors
Overseeing/analysing water utility investment plan/business plan

2.2 How many formal service providers operate in your city's administrative boundaries and are they managed by public and/or private operators?

Services	Number of service providers	Names of service providers	Operator status
Water supply			
Sanitation			

2.3 What are the various forms of water access/delivery in your city? ***Please use the drop-down menu provided to answer yes/no in the appropriate cell.***
In-house domestic connection
Yard-tap, shared connection
Public tap, stand-pipe
Decentralised provision through networks managed by communities
Boreholes, wells
Tanker trucks
Bottled water
Rainwater collection
Other, please specify which other form of sanitation facility:

2.4 What are the various forms of sanitation facilities in your city? ***Please use the drop-down menu provided to answer yes/no in the appropriate cell.***
Flush/pour-flush to piped sewer or septic tank or pit latrine
Flush/pour-flush to open drain
Ventilated improved pit latrine, pit latrine with slab
Open pit
Buckets
Hanging toilet/latrine
Other, please specify which other form of sanitation facility:

2.5 Does your city participate in the decision-making process of a river basin organisation? ***Please use the drop-down menu provided to answer yes/no in the appropriate cell.***

2.6 Which mechanisms, tools and institutions are used to co-ordinate water policy between your city and other levels of government (including other municipalities, regions or provinces)?
Inter-municipal co-operation
Subnational institution dealing specifically with water (e.g. river basin organisations, water agency, etc.)
Shared databases and information systems
Performance indicators
Co-ordination platforms between local and/or authorities and utilities
Other, please specify which other mechanisms:

2.7 Please select one of these co-ordination mechanisms that proved successful and explain briefly how it functions and its contribution to better urban water governance
Co-ordination mechanism:

2.8 In your country/state/region, is there a dedicated water and/or sanitation services regulatory agency? ***Please use the drop-down menu provided to answer in the appropriate cell.***

3. Policies

3.1 In your country, is there a dedicated national water policy, indicating goals, duties, resources needed? ***Please use the drop-down menu provided to answer yes/no in the appropriate cell.***

If yes, is the United Nations right to water and sanitation recognised in this law?
Please use the drop-down menu provided to answer yes/no in the appropriate cell.

3.2 Has your city developed a dedicated water and sanitation policy at the local level?

If yes, is such policy:

- Indicating clear goals?
- Indicating clear duties?
- Indicating resources needed?
- Including emergency strategies?
- Being regularly monitored?

3.3 Has your city developed an explicit water resources policy at the local level (targeting groundwater and freshwater at point source or catchment level)?

If yes, is such policy:

- Indicating clear goals?
- Indicating clear duties?
- Indicating resources needed?
- Including climate resilience aspects?
- Being regularly monitored?

3.4 At the city level, are there requirements/frameworks for prioritisation among water uses in case of scarcity or emergency situations? ***Please use the drop-down menu provided to answer in the appropriate cell.***

In case of prioritised allocation, please rank from 1 to 5:

- Domestic uses
- Industry
- Energy
- Irrigation and breeding
- Environmental sustainability

3.5 Does your city implement explicit measures at the local level to guarantee access to water and/or sanitation services to vulnerable groups, such as:

- Poor populations
- People living with disabilities
- Indigenous peoples and ethnic minorities
- Population living in informal settlements
- Women or female-headed household
- Other, please specify:

3.6 In your city, are all people guaranteed a minimum amount of water for their basic needs? ***Please use the drop-down menu provided to answer yes/no in the appropriate cell.***

3.7 At the city level, are there social measures for vulnerable categories of water and/or sanitation users?

If yes, please specify the nature of these measures:

- Social tariff
- Social connection rate
- Both
- Other, please specify which other social measure(s):

3.8 Which of the following mechanisms have been put in place at the city level to enhance transparency and integrity for water-related issues management:
Annual budget auditing of water and sanitation services, or municipal water-related spending
Annual disclosure of financial information of water and sanitation services
Clear budget transparency principles and rules applied
Anti-bribery management systems
Whistle-blower protection policies
Institutional anti-corruption plans, codes of conduct or integrity charters
Clear procurement processes
Random integrity testing or audits
Clear and mandatory processes to prevent potential conflict of interest
Other, please specify which other mechanism(s):

3.9 How important is the influence of the following policy areas on urban water management in your city?
Land use and spatial planning
Building codes and housing
Transportation
Solid waste management
Public health
Tourism
Manufacturing industry
Energy
Agriculture

4. Financing

4.1 At the level of your city, are there water- and sanitation-related investment plans and programmes? *Please use the drop-down menu provided to answer yes/no in the appropriate cell.*
If yes, do they guide decision-making in your city?

4.2 In your city, are water accounts separated from city accounts to ensure clear identification of water money revenues and spending? *Please use the drop-down menu provided to answer yes/no in the appropriate cell.*

4.3 In your city, the water supply and sanitation services are financed through: *Please use the drop-down menu provided to describe the importance of each funding source, in the appropriate cell.*
Sources of funding
Tariffs
Subsidies from the central, regional and/or local government
Financial transfer from international aid

4.4 Which of the following economic instruments are in place for water management in your city? *Please use the drop-down menu provided to answer yes/no in the appropriate cell.*
Bulk water tariffs
Retail water tariffs/user charges
Water abstraction charges
Water pollution (effluent) charges

Fines and penalties
Other, please, specify which other economic instruments:

4.5 Is there uniform guidance at the national or subnational levels to set tariffs, abstraction or pollution charges, or groundwater tax? *Please use the drop-down menu provided to answer yes/no in the appropriate cell.*

5. Stakeholder engagement

5.1 Did your city carry out a stakeholder mapping to make sure that all those that have a stake in the outcome or that are likely to be affected are clearly identified, and their responsibilities, core motivations and interactions understood? *Please use the drop-down menu provided to answer yes/no in the appropriate cell.*

5.2 Which categories of stakeholders are the most difficult to engage with?
Service providers and/or their national professional organisations
Regional/provincial government
Local government (other than your own municipality)
Inter-municipal/metropolitan authority
Central government
Subnational institution dealing specifically with water (e.g. river basin organisation, water agency, etc.)
Regulator
Business/Industry
Irrigators and their associations
Civil society, non-governmental organisations (NGOs)
Financial actors (donors, international financial institutions, investors)
Science, academia and research centres
Customers and their associations
Trade unions and workers
Advisors (e.g. engineering, consulting firms)
International organisations
Media
Vulnerable groups (e.g. poor populations, indigenous peoples, ethnic minorities, etc.)
Key local partners (e.g. village chief, community/neighbourhood or street leaders, etc.)

5.3 In your city, are there mechanisms to engage with the following groups regarding water-related topics:
Poor populations
People living with disabilities
Indigenous peoples and ethnic minorities
Population living in informal settlements
Women or female-headed household
Other, please specify which other group:

5.4 Which of the following mechanisms does your city mostly use to engage stakeholders in water-related decision-making?
Subnational institution dealing specifically with water (e.g. river basin organisations, water agency, etc.)
Associations of water utilities, water regulators, etc.
Survey/Polls/Referendum

Hotlines
Workshops
Meetings
Expert panels
Citizen committees
Traditional media (newspaper, newsletter, television, radio)
Web-based communication technologies (online platforms, email, social media, website, application, etc.)

5.5 Which of the following mechanisms are used to assess the performance of urban water management?
Survey, poll (households or citizens' satisfaction, etc.)
Benchmark
Evaluation report (effectiveness, efficiency, impact…)
Other, please specify which other mechanisms:

5.6 Which of the following obstacles mostly hinder stakeholder engagement in your city?
Consultation "capture" (lobbies, over-representation of certain categories, etc.)
Lack of funding to support stakeholder engagement
Lack of time and/or means (e.g. staff)
Lack of political will, commitment and/or leadership
Weak legal framework to support stakeholder engagement
Stakeholder consultation "fatigue" (difficulty to maintain motivation)
Political discontinuity (turnover of staff, shifting priorities, etc.)
Misaligned objectives of stakeholders
Resistance to change
Low capacity to engage in consultation (education, training)
Complexity of issues at hand
Geographical distance from decision-making cores (e.g. remote areas)
Decision-makers' fear of losing influence and power

6. Data, monitoring and evaluation

6.1 Does your city report data to the GLASS report and/or SDG-related monitoring?
If yes, please specify how the data are reported:

6.2 Are the following data on city water and sanitation services available at the local level in your city?
Cost of water services (transporting and supplying water; collecting and treating wastewater; staff cost, energy cost, etc.)
Cost recovery and prices in relation to consumer income and purchasing power
If yes, please indicate the average share of water invoice in household income (%)
Knowledge of assets, maintenance of infrastructure programmes to ensure sustainable operation, maintenance and renewal
Drinking water and wastewater quality controls against specified standards

6.3 Are the following data on risk management available at the local level for your city?
Projections/scenarios with reference to climate change and exposed lives and goods, risks of floods, drought and accidental pollution
Meteorological data, including data on rainfall

Data on water abstractions, flows and pressures
Historical data on water disasters
Data on vulnerability (human beings and properties)/exposure to risk

6.4 Are key data on water resources management being produced regularly at the city level? ***Please use the drop-down menu provided to answer yes/no in the appropriate cell.***
If yes, please specify if they are:
Part of a harmonised, integrated, standardised and co-ordinated information system across the country?
Publicly available and communicated to users?
If yes, please specify how they are communicated to users:

7. Obstacles

Which of the following obstacles continue to hinder water governance in your city?
Fragmentation of municipal authorities, and/or of service providers
Lack of staff (technical, managerial), knowledge and/or competency on water
Lack of funding (due to low tariffs, difficulties in collecting tariffs, affordability issues, etc.)
Low level of investment (due to weak prioritisation of investment, lack of multi-annual strategic plans and multi-annual budgets, etc.)
Competing water uses (agriculture, energy, households, etc.)
Incomplete, outdated and/or fragmented data
Lack of policy coherence (agriculture, health, energy, urban development, etc.)
Lack of river basin or catchment-oriented management
Lack of conflict resolution mechanism
Corruption and/or political interference
Weak or missing public procurement processes
Weak regulatory authorities and/or weak enforcement
Low citizen awareness and stakeholder engagement
Lack of monitoring and evaluation of public policies

8. Future priorities

Are any of the following actions contemplated to cope with future water challenges in your city? ***Please use the drop-down menu provided to answer yes/no in the appropriate cell.***
Strategies
Build, operate or maintain water infrastructure
Raise citizen awareness on water risks
Foster co-operation with cities and/or national government
Develop legal or regulatory frameworks
Enhance stakeholder engagement
Catalyse water financing
Build capacity of officials and stakeholders

www.ingramcontent.com/pod-product-compliance
Lightning Source LLC
LaVergne TN
LVHW081413110826
845149LV00010B/1727

* 9 7 8 9 2 6 4 3 5 9 6 2 8 *